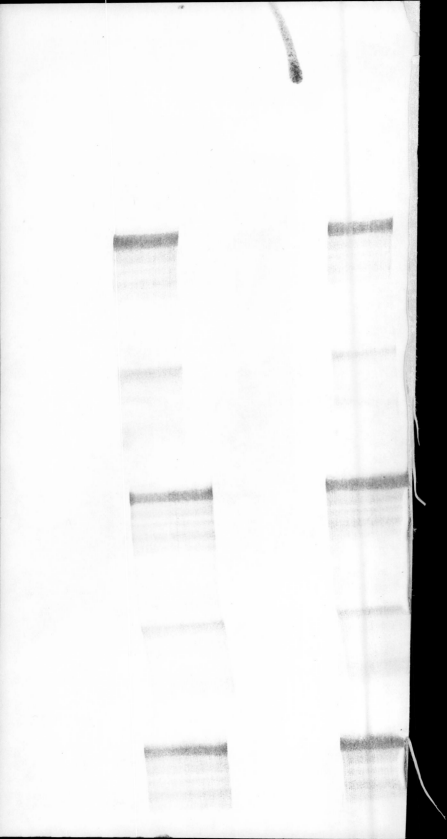

THE·LISTENER'S·GUIDE·TO
Folk Music

Sarah Lifton

Facts On File
119 West 57th Street, New York, N.Y. 10019

A Quarto Book

Copyright © 1983 by Quarto Marketing Ltd.

First published in the United States in 1983 by
Facts On File, Inc.
460 Park Avenue South
New York, New York 10016

Library of Congress Cataloging in Publication Data
Lifton, Sarah.
Listener's guide to folk music.

Includes index.
1. Folk music—History and criticism.   2. Music,
Popular (Songs, etc.)—History and criticism.
I. Title.
ML3545.L454   1983   781.7   82-15390

ISBN 0-87196-720-0

The Listener's Guide to Folk Music
was produced and prepared by
Quarto Marketing Ltd.
212 Fifth Avenue,
New York, New York 10010

Editor: **Gene Santoro**
Editorial Assistant: **Richard Selman**
Designer: **Richard Boddy**
Cover Design: **Abby Kagan**

Typesetting: B.P.E. Graphics Inc.
Printed and bound in the United States by
the Maple-Vail Group

C·O·N·T·E·N·T·S

**To the memory of
Gaye Tardy**

ACKNOWLEDGEMENTS

Many generous people gave freely of their time, resources and expertise as I was planning and writing this book: thanks especially to Howard and Roz Larman of Folkscene Productions, who offered extensive knowledge, advice and support, as well as gracious permission to reprint quotations from their excellent interviews with many of the artists; Marsha Necheles, who was more generous than I had any right to expect; Paulette Gershen, whose record collection and knowledge of Ireland greatly augmented my own; Sam Epstein, for his counsel and cooperation; Phyl Lobl, for extensive information on Australia (sadly, unused); Louis Killen for straightening me out on the origins of the English Revival; Ray Frank, Tom Barr, and Nancy Noennig, for their ideas and friendship; and most of all, Frank Scott, without whose constant help, guidance, and meticulous review of the manuscript I would have been unable to complete the project—even if I couldn't always follow his valuable advice. Thanks are also due the many record companies who made their products more readily available to me, and to the musicians, whose music has given me so many hours of pleasure. And special thanks go to Norman and Gene, supportive colleagues, who will do anything to get their names in print.

INTRODUCTION

"Folk music?" an intrigued relative inquired shortly after I had begun working on this book. "I just love Joan Baez."

I agreed that the 1960s folk queen had a beautiful voice, but explained that her music had little relation to the type I would be writing about.

"Then I guess I don't know what you mean by folk music," she replied, somewhat puzzled.

No, I suppose she didn't. And she's not alone. In fact, there are probably as many different explanations of what folk music is as there are people addressing the issue. Nineteenth-century scholars identified it as the songs and tunes of largely isolated, rural populations. The music was transmitted through an oral tradition, it was unauthored, and it changed over time and distance as succeeding generations and neighboring communities adapted it to fit their needs, through what has come to be called the "folk process."

To get an idea of what the folklorists meant, imagine an international, multigenerational game of "Telephone." Someone sings a song at a community gathering, perhaps a ballad about lost love; the next person who attempts to sing it forgets several words and makes up new ones on the spot. Someone else hears the revised version, then deliberately alters it to incorporate references to his recently departed sweetheart. Still another sings the song in his native dialect and changes the melody because some of the notes are too high for him to reach. And so on. Needless to say, in very short order the song is known in myriad versions, and it's anyone's guess which was the original. And it really doesn't matter.

With increased literacy and the advent of electronic recording the nature of folk music began to change. As an example of how, picture the following scene. Not long ago, I was present at a group singing session. The crowd was singing well-known "folk" songs, and as each new song was suggested, the room was filled with people frantically flipping through the pages of their songbooks so they could all sing exactly the same words to exactly the same melody, even when the song was widely known in many different versions. Of course, most of my companions were completely unaware of the existence of the other variants; the only ones they knew, and the ones they were adhering to so rigidly, had been made popular through records. So much for the personal touches.

That, naturally, is an extreme example. But many changes have taken place in folk music, and they are largely the result of the professional folk musician— stereotypically characterized as a limpid-eyed young man or woman with a guitar or banjo, singing love songs or topical songs. But for all his familiarity in the public consciousness, the professional folk musician is a relatively new animal, and something of a hybrid, drawing on the repertoire of the traditional musician and the role of the art singer. Of course, the stereotype bears little resemblance to the actual thing. But while such interpreters of folk music now form the core of the folk scene and for the most part are the people who are preserving the music in our own time, they are essentially entertainers, and their role only became defined during the folk "revival" of the 1940s, 1950s, and 1960s. For this reason, they are often referred to as revival musicians.

Traditional, or source, musicians, on the other hand, are the real thing, as defined by our 19th-century forebears. They are the musicians who grew up with the musical traditions they are perpetuating. They may have lived in a region where traditional music was still an important part of everyday life, or they may be the children of traditional musicians, who in turn passed the music on to them. Generally, traditional musicians are not professional musicians, although there are some exceptions, and these days they will often receive compensation for their performances. In most cases they are at least as accomplished as the revival musicians. But you can't apply the same aesthetic to their music that you would to their professional counterparts. Many of the techniques of the traditional musician sound rougher than modern ears are accustomed to. Traditional singers, for example, often change the tempo or rhythm of a verse, or even change the melody, if they feel the material warrants it. Similarly, the instrumentalist may explore the areas between the notes on the diatonic scale—the so-called blue notes associated with jazz and the blues—which may simply sound out of tune to someone weaned on commercial music. Traditional styles are highly individual, and what signals a superb performance by a traditional musician are the emotions the performer both conveys himself and elicits in the listener.

By now you might be wondering where songwriters fit into all this. Or even if they fit in at all, for songwriters do indeed occupy a sort of no-man's land in the realm of folk music. Although, obviously, all folk music was at one time composed by someone, the anonymity factor that figures so prominently in the conventional definition of folk music is missing with the folk-oriented songwriter. Yet a number of songwriters continue to produce new music firmly rooted in the folk idiom. Sometimes their songs are mistaken for traditional ones; other times, the songs are absorbed into the tradition, subjected to the changes of the folk process. Often their songs are clearly contemporary but simply appeal to the "folk aesthetic."

And that aesthetic, and the attitude behind it, are at the heart of the folk scene today. Many musicians playing the folk clubs wouldn't meet the criteria folklorists use to identify folk musicians, but they appeal to the same people who love traditional music. One quality they tend to share is a noncommercial approach toward their music. That doesn't mean they don't care whether or not they're paid for performing. Obviously, they do. But perhaps the point is best made by observing that many folk musicians make their living by some means other than music. And you can be sure that those who do rely entirely on their music for their income would be playing the same kind of material for pleasure even if they were working in an office. As an aesthetic, folk music is harder to pin down. Certainly there are many mainstream musicians whose material reflects folk influences. But there is a simple eloquence to folk music, no matter how complex its arrangements. No matter how well-rehearsed or how polished a performance, between the notes you can hear the honest, rougher edges of the traditional source.

Equally important in identifying folk music, new or old, is its subject matter. Folk music deals with the concerns of everyday life—love, work, politics, current events, human relations, death, tragedy, customs, and so on. It speaks to all walks of life and confronts all aspects of human experience. Perhaps most significant, it offers reassuring evidence that people in times past had the same concerns we do, and dealt with them in much the same way.

Because folk music encompasses so many different kinds of subjects and such a wide array of musical styles, it comes closer to offering something for everyone than perhaps any other category of music. This very diversity, however, is most troublesome when compiling a book like this one, with severe space restrictions. In selecting the musicians to include and the records to review here, I've tried to choose people whose music has fairly broad appeal within the Anglo, American, and Celtic traditions. As a result, this volume is something like a musical wine-tasting. At a wine-tasting, you get to sample a few wines, perhaps several varieties by several vintners. You know there are a great many more available, and if you discover one you like, you might be prompted to try other similar wines.

This book functions in much the same way. At best, I can present only a smattering of the staggering amount of folk music available on record. I've tried to include several influential traditional musicians in each chapter, and some outstanding revivalists and folk-oriented songwriters currently on the scene. In general, I've forsaken the well-known, popular figures with acknowledged folk roots in favor of the lesser-known musicians who currently have stronger ties to traditional music. You don't need a book, for example, to tell you that Gordon Lightfoot was influenced by traditional ballads. On the other hand, some forms of traditional music may be an acquired taste, so I've tried to select performers whose music and presentation are accessible to the modern listener unacquainted with the various traditions. As you become more familiar with folk music, you might want to subscribe to the publications listed in the back; they'll give you a broader and more up-to-date idea of the music that is being produced.

I've made every effort to list records that are still in print. But there's no way to guarantee that they will remain available indefinitely. Where albums have been released on different labels in the US and UK or Ireland, the label listed first refers to the country under discussion. In the back of the book you'll find mail-order sources for the records; they're invaluable if your local record stores can't be induced to stock folk music.

Because of the international scope of the book, the material is organized geographically primarily for convenience. But you should be aware that there is tremendous overlap between traditions, and often the music doesn't fit neatly into a single category. You should also know that there are active revivals currently under way in Canada, Australia, and in many European countries but space prevented a discussion of them here. The mail-order distributors can help you obtain their records as well.

The pages that follow can only hint at the wealth of material available to anyone interested in folk music. Some of the best music being produced today, in fact, never makes it into a concert hall or onto record. It is produced by people like you and me—people who love the music so much that the most satisfying way of enjoying it is by creating it ourselves. You don't have to be a professional-caliber musician or buy an expensive instrument to have fun participating. Learn to play spoons. Buy a jews harp or a tin whistle. You'll quickly find that listening to folk music is only half the picture.

Whether you play music yourself or just play records, though, I hope you'll detect some of the vitality that has injected folk music with such remarkable longevity, that has prompted succeeding generations to embrace it as enthusiastically as their predecessors did, that has made it some of the most beautiful, affecting and entertaining music ever played. If you discover a tradition you like—and it's hard to imagine that you won't—don't be afraid to explore it in greater depth.

ENGLAND

England's musical heritage is rich and textured, marked by a varied and vital tradition. In his acclaimed survey of English folk music, *Folk Song in England*, the noted musicologist A.L. Lloyd described English folk song as "the musical and poetic expression of the fantasy of the lower classes." And as such it has served many purposes in the communities in which it came to play, not the least of which is reinforcing the sense of community itself. For folk music in England, as elsewhere, has always been a group activity, whether it's a singer entertaining his mates in a pub or a band providing accompaniment for a country dance.

Folk music has been an integral part of cultural life since before the Middle Ages. Even today, in fact, vestiges of pre-Christian culture remain evident. Among the many types of traditional songs and dance in England are those pertaining to ceremony and ritual. Many of these, such as wassail songs (midwinter carols), May songs (celebratings of spring), harvest and Halloween songs are carryovers from paganism, when magic was invoked to mobilize the forces of nature to ensure a bountiful harvest. Later people, no less dependent on nature for survival, retained the customs, and Christianity eventually adopted them and invested them with Christian trappings and significance. Their origins in paganism weren't entirely obscured, however. The celebration of Christ's birth, for example, was set in December because the early church was unable to deter the populace from its traditional midwinter celebrations.

Other types of traditional song served more as entertainment. Sometimes referred to as the "big ballads," these were often lengthy narratives recounting events centering around magic, tragedy, love, or scandal. Later ballads tended to be more romantic, when relating to love, or even bawdy; other popular topics included the social ills of the day, such as impressment and deportation. An important influence on folk songs from the mid-15th century on came in the form of broadsides, printed flyers that were sold on the streets. These often lurid accounts of events of the day, such as murders or hangings, were popular at all levels of society; students at the universities were often avid collectors of the sheets. But with the advent of newspapers in the 18th century, broadsides became the domain of the lower classes.

Other traditions developed around work. Best known were sea shanteys—the songs sailors sang aboard ship in order to accomplish tasks that required precision teamwork. And, as the Industrial Revolution increasingly came to dominate people's lives, songs began to emerge relating to the effects the new technology had on the work and way of life of ordinary people. One well-known example, "The Weaver and the Factory Maid," reflected the pressures industrialization placed on interpersonal relations, specifically the love of a weaver for a factory worker, considered an inappropriate alliance.

Dance provided another fertile source of traditional music. Country dance, which had long played a role in rural communities, was a social activity. In the north, hornpipes, jigs, and reels dominated the scene, while in the south the emphasis was on polkas. Morris dancing and other ritual dances, like the ceremonial songs, recalled pagan times.

Much of the traditional singing style was unaccompanied, and so it remains today—the result of the Reformation, when musical instruments were condemned as evil. In an attempt to compensate for the lack of accompaniment, singers developed vocal techniques that embellished the melodies. These embellishments, which can still be heard in traditional and traditional-style singing, are called ornaments or decoration, and consist of everything from a bleating sound, to grace notes, to variations in the melody, tempo, and rhythm of the song to suit the material. English music tends to be less ornamented than either Scottish or Irish, but the extent depends on the singer and style.

Of course, accompanied singing is an integral part of the folk scene today. The guitar is the instrument most commonly associated with the genre, but historically its connection with traditional music is tenuous at best. Originally the guitar was a genteel instrument of the upper classes, found often in afternoon musicales held in the parlors of well-bred people. Traditional music leaned toward the fiddle; the Northumbrian smallpipes (in the north); the melodeon (a button accordion) and, eventually, the concertina, which found its way down from the upper classes; the banjo; the mandolin; the hammered dulcimer; and finally the guitar. Today virtually any instrument can be used in traditional music, either as accompaniment to singing or as part of a band. (Sue Harris has even made the oboe an accepted part of the folk scene.)

During the 19th century, industrialization began to encroach on rural life, and society became increasingly fragmented; the rural tradition and, eventually the urban one as well, began to fade. It is largely due to the folk song collectors—upper-class ladies and gentlemen who sought to preserve the music—that the current revival of interest in traditional song and dance ever took place at all.

The Collectors

Although folk music has conventionally been associated with the lower and working classes, its largely rural orientation has not precluded an interest by the upper classes. As early as the 17th century, upper-class gentlemen were engaged in collecting ballads. Samuel Pepys himself collected over 1600 ballads, although like most of his fellow collectors, his interest in the songs was purely literary.

By far the most important and influential collection of British ballads, however, was that published between 1882 and 1898 by Harvard professor Francis James Child, under the title *English and Scottish Popular Ballads*. Child's work was unique in its exploration of the variants of the ballad themes, and its study of the relationship between ballads of different cultures. The Child ballads were so significant that to this day many of the songs are referred to by the number Child assigned them in his collection. Like the other collectors of his day, however, Child's interest in the ballads was exclusively with the words, and it wasn't until Bertrand Bronson published his *Traditional Tunes of the Child Ballads* between 1959 and 1972 that the lyrics were reunited with their melodies.

Around the turn of the century, a whole new breed of collector emerged. They believed that traditional music was moribund, and that they were preserving its last vestiges for posterity. In 1898 the Folk Song Society was formed to promote the study of traditional songs, and its membership grew to 110 in its first year.

September 1903, however, marked one of the turning points in folk song collecting of the period and, indeed, of the early decades of this century. Cecil Sharp, vacationing in Somerset, heard a man named John English sing a folk song. Taken with the song, Sharp recorded the words and music, added harmony, and accompanied its performance that night by the church choir. Sharp loved the music he discovered, devoting his life to its collection and promotion.

Sharp and his cohorts restricted their efforts to rural song, ignoring entirely the industrial ballads that sprang up in response to the Industrial Revolution. And most of the singers they met were old, reinforcing their perception that the tradition was nearly extinct.

If the collectors of Sharp's day had a major failing, it was their attempt to make the folk song tradition fit their preconceived notions. Sharp, for example, believed that the ballad tradition was unaccompanied; therefore, when he visited Appalachia, A. L. Lloyd said, the people hid their banjos and guitars. It was a similar perspective that caused Sharp to ignore the urban manifestations of the folk process. He and his fellow collectors viewed the folk song tradition as a dying curiosity rather than a living tradition.

Around the same time another group of people was becoming interested in folk music, only they were drawn to the tradition for different reasons. The English composers Ralph Vaughan Williams, Gustav Holst, Percy Grainger, George Butterworth, E. J. Moeran, and Herbert Hughes were looking to folk music for inspiration and raw material, and Holst, Butterworth, and Williams all produced works from their own collections.

World War I put a stop to collecting for a time, and although E. J. Moeran discovered Harry Cox in 1921, no major advances were made in the field until the 1950s, when the seeds of the folk revival began to germinate.

Roots of the Revival

The birth of the post-World War II folk music revival in England is largely the story of three men: Alan Lomax, of the Archive of Folk Music at the Library of Congress; Ewan MacColl; and A. L. Lloyd. Lomax, MacColl has said, was the great catalyst of the revival. He was in Britain putting together a series of folk music programs for the BBC when he met both MacColl and Lloyd. Lomax's genius was for bringing people together, and this he did with MacColl and Lloyd, observing that the two men were from similar backgrounds and shared a similar perspective and strong interest in folk music.

Ewan MacColl

MacColl, whose real name is Jimmy Miller, grew up the son of Scottish parents in England. His mother was a fine traditional singer, and MacColl has attributed many of his songs to his father as well. He began writing songs while still a boy and became politically active at the age of 14.

MacColl's political interests led him to a series of street theaters and left-wing theater groups. He and his fellow performers often put new words to old ballads and sang them to their audiences, which sometimes numbered thousands of people. Around 1949 or 1950, MacColl's Theatre Workshop was putting on a ballad opera, and Alan Lomax came to see MacColl. The meeting with Lomax changed the course of his career, for it was through Lomax that he became involved in the BBC's folk music program.

PHOTO BY SARAH LIFTON

Ewan MacColl, along with his wife Peggy Seeger, has been behind many early milestones in the English revival.

A. L. Lloyd

A. L. Lloyd was born in England, but when he was in his mid-teens, his parents died, and he was sent to Australia, where he remained for nine years, working on a cattle station in the bush. Although he had little formal education, he had an insatiable thirst for knowledge, and he borrowed books through the mail from the library. He bought a portable gramophone and listened to classical records but was equally intrigued by the songs his coworkers or the shearers would sing, and tried to learn those he liked.

In time Lloyd returned to England, which was still caught in the throes of the Depression. Work was scarce, so he went to sea, working in the whaling industry. Late in 1938 he heard a broadcast on the BBC about unemployment in the United States. He suggested to the BBC that they do a similar program focusing on Britain, especially life at sea, from the laborers' point of view. Lloyd was approached to write the program himself, and when it met with acclaim, he was offered a contract to continue writing for the BBC, which he accepted.

While at sea, Lloyd had been exposed to many different kinds of music, and after World War II, working as a journalist, he used the opportunity to explore many indigenous musical forms. He became well versed in the music of Eastern Europe and South America and eventually turned his attention to the traditional music of England.

"Ballads and Blues"

Although as early as 1942 the radio program "Country Magazine" had featured a traditional song every week, Alan Lomax couldn't help noticing that the British music scene was dominated by young English kids playing American music, ignoring their own heritage. At Lomax's prodding, the BBC began to finance the collection of English folk songs, and Lomax, MacColl, and Lloyd set out to introduce British youth to their rich native tradition, by making use of the mass media. In 1951 they emerged with a series of radio programs called *Ballads and Blues*, featuring musicians from a variety of cultures:

Lloyd represented England; MacColl, Scotland; and various Americans from Big Bill Broonzy to Jean Ritchie and Lomax himself represented the United States. Each would present the regional variant of a song on a common topic, reinforcing the idea that there was an equally vital English counterpart to the American music. The response from the listeners was unprecedented for a music program on the BBC. After the initial 6 shows had run, they were repeated, 4 more were produced, and the show was moved to the prime-time Saturday evening slot. The audience grew to over 14 million, and at that point the folk music revival was launched.

And around the same time, the skiffle movement was gaining momentum. Skiffle was a musical style based primarily on black American traditions, although Uncle Dave Macon and Woody Guthrie also provided inspiration. Its most visible manifestation was Lonnie Donegan's rendition of Leadbelly's "Rock Island Line," which became a hit in Britain in 1956 and spawned numerous imitators. Skiffle ran out of steam after about two years, driven under partly by the entrance of commercial interests into the sphere. Yet its appeal was unmistakable: rather than a music created by adults in the music industry, here was a music in which youth of the day could participate. Guitar sales skyrocketed, and interest in traditional music—American and British—grew.

By 1956 the folk club scene was also beginning to flourish. Tucked away in rooms off pubs, groups of people began to gather to share folk music, although their tastes at the time were catholic, to say the least. Once again MacColl was in the foreground of the picture, having formed one of England's first folk clubs—the Ballads and Blues Club—in 1953.

At the end of the decade, MacColl was again approached to produce a radio program. He was asked to focus on the story of John Axon, a railroadman who had been killed while attempting to prevent a collision. Axon's was an exceptional act of heroism, and MacColl and producer Charles Parker traveled to the depot where Axon had worked to interview people who had known him. They recorded the material on tape, and MacColl wrote songs based on the words of the people they had spoken with. The songs were linked by portions of the recorded interviews, and the result was the first of the "radio ballads," a series of 8 documentaries about different segments of the British population. Many well-known people collaborated with MacColl and Parker on the project, including A. L. Lloyd, Peggy Seeger (MacColl's wife), Seamus Ennis, Louis Killen, and Dave Swarbrick, and many of MacColl's best and most memorable songs were those he wrote for the radio ballads.

Yet another of MacColl's experiments also had far-reaching influence. Put off by the international blend of songs that dominated the folk clubs, sung largely by British people, he issued a dictum at his own club that singers could perform only the material of their native lands. The response was immediate—and hostile. The Ballad and Blues Club, which had enjoyed turnaway crowds, suddenly went begging for an audience. After about 3 months, the audience began to trickle back, and the policy not only created better-informed audiences, but prompted singers to learn new material.

The clubs, in fact, became a major force on the scene, whether engaging in restrictive policies like MacColl's, or offering more latitude. Many clubs even set up archives of tapes, where people could go to hear traditional material sung by traditional musicians. The effect was to bring the revival closer to traditional sources.

Continuing Influence

While the influence of Ewan MacColl and his followers is greatly diminished on the current folk scene, he remains a significant presence. Many of his songs, such as "Shoals of Herring," "Thirty-Foot Trailer," "Freeborn Man," "Manchester Rambler," and "The First Time Ever I Saw Your Face" are still being performed and recorded, and he and Peggy Seeger make regular concert appearances. MacColl's somewhat academic style of singing, primarily unaccompanied, has fallen out of favor, but his reputation as someone unafraid of controversy has endured, and he is universally acknowledged as one of the seminal figures of the English folk revival.

MacColl may have been the visible, public figure in the early days of the revival, but A. L. Lloyd, who died in September 1982, was nonetheless an equally important force. In 1952 he produced a collection of industrial ballads called *Come All Ye Bold Miners;* the existence of this music had escaped public notice, as the collectors up to that point had devoted themselves to preserving the rural music. In 1959 he coedited with Ralph Vaughan Williams *The Penguin Book of English Folk Songs.* The impact of its publication was enormous, as it provided fledgling singers with a source of new material. In 1967 he produced *Folk Song in England,* the first major analytical work on the subject, and a book of tremendous influence.

Lloyd was an excellent singer, with a style similar to MacColl's but more relaxed. His major influence, however, was as a scholar. Entirely self-taught, he was perhaps the leading student of English folk music, a renowned author, and a well-loved and highly respected figure.

S·E·L·E·C·T·E·D   R·E·C·O·R·D·I·N·G·S

Ewan MacColl (with Peggy Seeger)
Cold Snap
(FOLKWAYS FW 8765)
•
The Jacobite Rebellions
(TOPIC 12T79)
•
By Other Artists:
The Songs of Ewan MacColl
(RUBBER 027)

Cold Snap is a characteristic collection of traditional and contemporary ballads sung by MacColl and Peggy Seeger. *The Jacobite Rebellions* presents excellent arrangements and singing. *The Songs of Ewan MacColl* features Dick Gaughan, Tony Capstick, and Dave Burland, and showcases MacColl's songwriting talents, even though he doesn't sing on the the record.

A. L. Lloyd:
First Person
(TOPIC 12T118)

Lloyd was a tasteful and lively singer. With Dave Swarbrick on fiddle and Alf Edwards on concertina, this record makes for enjoyable listening, and the extensive liner notes are a mini-folklore course in themselves.

Source Singers

One of the main benefits of the folk revival has been the rediscovery of traditional, or source, singers and the notoriety they have received. Tucked away in fairly isolated communities, these musicians would have escaped notice altogether, and their music would probably have died away had not a public tired of the commercial pap they were being fed seized upon these last remaining links with the past and preserved their music, both by recording it and learning it.

Because industrialization has taken over more and more of the countryside, and isolated communities increasingly have become a thing of the past, fewer ties with the older traditions remain. For this reason, most of the traditional singers who have been captured on record are old; many are already dead. Although the best revival singers continue to look to traditional sources for both material and inspiration, folk fans in general have been sadly remiss about supporting traditional musicians, either by buying their records or attending their concerts. It seldom pays a record company to release an album by a traditional singer today, and few do. The loss will be ours if we don't learn to value the real article over an imitator, however polished and pretty.

S·E·L·E·C·T·E·D R·E·C·O·R·D·I·N·G·S

Folk Songs of Britain
(10 VOLS.)
(TOPIC 12T157-98)

An important collection of field recordings of traditional singers throughout Britain and Ireland. Each volume centers around a single theme, such as songs of ceremony, songs of animals, and so on. The finest traditional singers of Britain are represented, sometimes only in fragments of songs in order to accommodate the vast amount of material that has been included. An indispensable part of any collection of British and Irish traditional music.

Harry Cox

More than probably any other source singer, Harry Cox provided a fertile source of inspiration and material during the early years of the folk revival.

Cox, a farm laborer, was born in 1885 near Yarmouth in Norfolk. He learned many of his songs from his father, tagging along after him much of his childhood and even accompanying him into the pubs, where the older man would sing and play fiddle. Cox himself began singing in pubs at the age of 11, when he was cajoled into singing for the gatherings. As he grew older, he gradually developed a reputation as a singer, and was in constant demand for a song among his mates in the pubs.

In 1921 Cox was visited by the composer E.J. Moeran, who collected several songs from him, and in 1921 and 1931 several of Cox's songs were published in the *Folk Song Journal.* During the 1930s he made a record for the English Folk Dance and Song Society, and in 1942 he was visited by Francis Collinson, who was collecting material for the BBC radio program "Country Magazine." Cox's songs subsequently were published in the 1946 *Folk Song Journal* and in several collections of folk songs, and he was included in the BBC's folk music recording program.

Cox's singing style was very straightforward and at first may seem colorless when compared with the vibrant style of, say, Sam Larner; but its subtleties require repeated listenings to appreciate. Perseverance is rewarded, however, for Cox employed many of the traditional singer's devices effectively, if quietly, and produced many moving performances.

S·E·L·E·C·T·E·D R·E·C·O·R·D·I·N·G

Traditional English Love Songs
(FOLK-LEGACY FSB-20)

Released in 1964, this album is probably the only readily available recording of Cox's singing. It includes his versions of several well-known songs, along with many lesser-known ones.

Sam Larner

He was already a very old man (79) when first recorded, so it requires a little imagination to consider this fine singer as he must have been at his prime; yet Sam Larner has left an indelible mark on the world of folk music. A source of inspiration for numerous revival singers from Ewan MacColl and Louis Killen to Peter Bellamy, he had a repertoire of over 65 songs when he was "discovered" by BBC producer Phillip Donnellan in 1957.

Born in 1878, Larner was a native of Winterton in the county of Norfolk, one of 9 children of a fisherman. At the age of 8, he began making occasional sea voyages, and from 12 years old on, he spent much of his time aboard sailing vessels, searching out shoals of herring. In 1899 he made his first voyage aboard a steam-powered boat and continued serving aboard steam vessels until ill health forced his retirement in 1933. From then on, he made his living however he could.

Larner began singing in public at the age of 9, performing for pennies from visitors passing through Winterton. Later he sang at concerts and, of course, in the local pubs that he frequented when he came home from sea. Larner was well known locally as a singer, but it wasn't until Donnellan encountered him that he became known to the rest of the world. In 1957 he gave a concert in London; two months later, on his 80th birthday, he gave another concert to a sellout crowd. The highlight of the event was the sight of the 80-year-old man leading 500 young people in the chorus of "Maids, When You're Young Never Wed an Old Man."

Between 1957 and 1960, Larner was recorded several times, first by Donnellan, then by Peggy Seeger and Ewan MacColl. During the summer of 1960, Ewan MacColl and Charles Parker presented the radio ballad "Singing the Fishing," which focused on the fishermen of East Anglia and centered around Larner himself. MacColl's classic song, "Shoals of Herring," was written for and about Larner for this broadcast.

Larner's singing was characterized by remarkable spirit and good humor. He clearly enjoyed his songs and singing; frequently he would dissolve into laughter at a line or verse, and occasionally he would pause at the end of a verse or between songs to explain some point that contributed to the understanding of the material. Larner died in 1965, and although his legacy is carried on by a number of revival singers, their version is only a pale copy of the original.

S·E·L·E·C·T·E·D R·E·C·O·R·D·I·N·G·S

A Garland for Sam
(TOPIC 12T244)

Now Is the Time for Fishing
(FOLKWAYS FG 3507)

Both these albums date from the period between 1957 and 1960. The Topic release contains recordings made by Phillip Donnellan; the Folkways record was edited by Peggy Seeger and Ewan MacColl. Although both albums present a fair sampling of Larner's singing, *Now Is the Time for Fishing* is both more informative and more interesting, as it includes Larner speaking as well as singing and offers insights into the man and his personality. Those who find speech intrusive on record may prefer the Topic release, however.

The Copper Family

In the midst of a tradition that folklorists once thought consisted exclusively of solo unaccompanied singing, the Copper Family is set apart from other source singers by the fact that they sing in harmony, in set arrangements that have existed in the family for at least 6 generations. Residing in and around Rottingdean in Sussex for over 200 years, they have had a tremendous influence on the folk revival and on people's perceptions of traditional song.

As early as 1898 the Coppers were known to folklorists, as they were visited by Mrs. Kate Lee, who in turn presented a paper to the Folk Song Society in 1899 and sang several of the songs she had collected from the members of the family then active, Thomas and James, known as "Brasser."

Around the middle of this century, the Copper Family was visited by Francis Collinson, who noticed Brasser's sons, Jim and John. Seamus Ennis recorded Jim and John for the BBC, and in 1950 Jim and his son Bob appeared on the BBC radio program "Country Magazine." Ennis and Peter Kennedy also recorded Bob and his cousin Ron for the BBC. During the heyday of the folk revival, the Copper Family consisted of Bob and Ron Copper, who died in 1978, and Bob's son and daughter, John and Jill.

The Coppers themselves have always had a profound feeling for the tradition they are upholding. In 1922 Brasser began writing out the family's songs, in response to the request of a farmer he had been working for. The task was continued and completed by Brasser's son Jim (father of Bob, who currently has possession of the book). Bob Copper himself is an articulate chronicler and has documented his family's contribution to traditional music in three books, including the prize-winning *A Song for Every Season* (so titled because the family has always had specific songs for specific occasions).

A.L. Lloyd once wrote that the Coppers' style probably reflects the survival of a musical form that at one time was more widespread in England. That style is sophisticated musically and demonstrates little of the "spontaneity" that traditional musicians are supposed to exhibit: the late Ron Copper learned the bass parts to the songs by rote. In fact, many traditional singers rehearse exhaustively, and this element is perhaps most audible in the Copper Family's singing.

The Coppers' impact on the folk revival has been enormous. Groups like the Young Tradition were strongly influenced by both their arrangements and repertoire, and many of the Copper Family's songs have become very well known and widely disseminated. The Copper Family themselves are perhaps easier for modern ears to accept than many traditional singers are because their use of harmony recalls musical styles more common in contemporary and classical music.

As pleasing as their music is, however, one of the most impressive qualities of the Copper Family remains their awareness that they are the keepers of something precious. As performers, they are compelling singers. And as a link with the past, they are an invaluable resource.

S·E·L·E·C·T·E·D R·E·C·O·R·D·I·N·G·S

A Song for Every Season
(LEADER LEAB 404) (4-RECORD SET)
•
Bob and Ron Copper:
English Shepherd and Farming Songs
(FOLK-LEGACY FSB-19)

Both of these albums are essential listening for lovers of English traditional music. *A Song for Every Season* by its very size is able to explore the family's music in greater depth than the Folk-Legacy release, but its availability may be erratic. For the timid, it is also available in an abridged version, on a single disc (Leader LED 2067). Although *English Shepherd and Farming Songs* includes only Bob and Ron Copper, it is nonetheless a pleasing recording, and one on which you are apt to find a satisfying mix of songs now standard in the revival, along with lesser-known ones.

Revival Singers

By far the most visible and popular of the musicians called "folk singers," the folk song interpreters, or revival singers, have started, in most cases, with a love for the music and respect for the old traditions; many then go on to add modern influences to the older ones, creating what can only be called a continuing tradition.

Revival singers often assume multiple identities: some, like Martin Carthy, not only perform solo and with bands but are brilliant instrumentalists as well. Others, like Ewan MacColl, can be considered both traditional and revival singers as well. Still others, like Peter Bellamy (and MacColl), have made names for themselves as songwriters as well as singers.

Likewise, there are as many different approaches to their material as there are singers. Vin Garbutt is wildly exuberant; Shirley Collins is subtle. Generally, however, the music of revival singers is more accessible to modern ears than that of traditional singers, even though the best revivalists try to maintain close ties with their traditional sources.

Martin Carthy

It's a long way from skiffle to the pinnacle of the folk revival. And it is, likewise, a long way from the early days of Martin Carthy's career to his current position of prominence. For Carthy is probably the leading male singer of the English folk revival, a spot he's earned through a combination of talent, innovation, experimentation, and respect for tradition.

As a child Carthy was a church choirboy, and his mother had been involved in the earlier folk revival that centered around Cecil Sharp, but like so many of his generation, he came to traditional music through the skiffle movement, and then the work of Ewan MacColl, A.L. Lloyd, and Alan Lomax. Early visits to the folk clubs gradually drew him into the mainstream of the folk scene; he learned to fingerpick the guitar and was a member of several groups, including the Three City Four, whose members included Leon Rosselson and Roy Bailey.

After leaving the group, Carthy performed alone for a while, then teamed up with fiddler Dave Swarbrick, making several memorable records. After another spell on his own, he joined Steeleye Span, his first foray into electric folk. He stayed with Steeleye for two albums, but left because of artistic differences, and his departure was reflected in the group's later work, which grew steadily more rock oriented.

After another stint on his own, Carthy joined the electric Albion Band, again leaving after a time to work on his own. In 1973 he joined the re-formed Watersons (Norma Waterson is his wife), maintaining his solo career as well, a dual identity that he still retains, even as he rejoined Steeleye briefly and, most recently, teamed up with John Kirkpatrick.

Clearly Carthy has not shied away from new directions, yet all the while he has retained a firm grip on the traditional aesthetic, always choosing tasteful material and singing it in a deeply affecting manner. He looks for material that has a contemporary message, although his repertoire is mainly traditional. Like many revivalists, he will take liberties with traditional songs if he feels another tune or different words would better suit the song, and many of his songs—often the ones that have come to be firmly associated with him—are such hybrids.

His clean-sounding, slightly nasal voice is augmented by a natural vibrato, and although at various times in his career he has sung in a highly mannered style, incorporating a great

PHOTO BY SARAH LIFTON

Martin Carthy, the leading male English vocalist, is as well known for his unusual guitar style as for his outstanding singing.

deal of ornamentation, more recently he has returned to a simpler vocal style. He is a compelling live performer, and the opportunity to see him in concert should not be missed, as he is highly informed about his material, and brings the songs vividly to life.

Carthy tends to dismiss the impact he has had on the folk revival, yet his influence is undeniable. In addition to providing a role model for many singers, and proving that it is possible to experiment with electric folk without sacrificing musical integrity, he evolved an altogether new guitar style, an accomplishment that is particularly important when one considers that until he developed it, the main influences on British guitar playing had been American. He uses many open tunings, but most significant is the sound he produces—staccato, highly rhythmic and percussive, with a drone and the melody line of the song carried in the bass. It is a very strong style, well suited to the modal melodies of many traditional songs, and one has only to listen to the playing of many other figures on the folk scene to realize its influence.

S·E·L·E·C·T·E·D   R·E·C·O·R·D·I·N·G·S

With Dave Swarbrick:
Prince Heathen
(TOPIC 12TS344)
·
Landfall
(TOPIC 12TS345)
·
Because It's There
(TOPIC 12TS389; ROUNDER 3031)
·
Out of the Cut
(TOPIC 12TS426)

The fact that all of these records are typical Carthy says a lot about the depth and versatility of his music. *Prince Heathen,* one of several collaborations with Dave Swarbrick, is a collection of traditional songs. Particularly noteworthy are the title tune and "Reynardine," which demonstrate Carthy's genius for retaining the original feeling of the material while employing contemporary arrangments. "Reynardine," in particular, has never sounded so sinister. Like *Prince Heathen, Landfall* is dominated by traditional material, but here Carthy has added three contemporary tunes as well; his version of the traditional "Cold Haily Windy Night" is a classic. *Because It's There* is sheer pleasure. Joined on several tracks by John Kirkpatrick, Carthy is at his liveliest. *Out of the Cut,* however, may be Carthy's best album yet; it's certainly his most political. Again with John Kirkpatrick on several cuts, he has created a remarkably varied and always entertaining assemblage of songs. Not only isn't there a bad track; there isn't even a mediocre one.

Peter Bellamy

Without a doubt, Peter Bellamy is an acquired taste. And where he goes, controversy is apt to follow. From his early days as part of the acclaimed trio, the Young Tradition, up to the present, he has developed a reputation as a flamboyant, opinionated singer with a reverence for tradition and at the same time an appetite for the new.

Bellamy grew up in rural Norfolk, coming initially to traditional music through the revival, and an attraction to Leadbelly. As he became aware of the English tradition, he began listening to Ewan MacColl, A.L. Lloyd, and Louis Killen, and then to traditional musicians. Sam Larner in particular, has had a profound influence on him.

It was as a member of the influential trio, the Young Tradition, which sang unaccompanied and in harmony, Copper-family style, that Bellamy first came to the forefront of the folk revival. He was the group's most visible (and audible) member and brought to their music a love of traditional material and the desire to perform it in a manner consistent with its origins.

He developed a highly mannered style of singing, characterized by profuse ornamentation and derived from a variety of sources, including traditional and revival singers of Britain, Ireland, and the United States. As he once put it, "Some of us

God did not give a very nice voice to, so what we've had to do is be interesting."

Indeed Bellamy's voice is far from euphonious, tending instead to be harsh-sounding and incorporating the traditional singer's "bleating" more than many singers do. In recent years it has mellowed, as Bellamy has reduced and integrated better the mannerisms that can make his singing intrusive, but a new listener could be put off by his style.

As important a revival singer as Bellamy is, however, it is most likely that other projects that he has been involved in will have the greatest impact. He has set to music about 100 of Rudyard Kipling's poems. Sometimes employing traditional melodies, sometimes making up his own, he has sensed in Kipling's work strong ties with traditional music.

Bellamy's greatest work to date, however, has been the composition and production of a remarkable ballad opera, *The Transports,* based on the true story of the first convicts transported to Australia. The album of the opera features leading members of the folk revival, including Martin Carthy, Nic Jones, Mike and Norma Waterson, Cyril Tawney, A.L. Lloyd, and June Tabor, with arrangements by Dolly Collins. Because Bellamy tires of projects quickly, he wrote the songs for the opera in about 4 days. Since the release of the recording in 1977, *The Transports* has been performed in public, and many of the songs are finding their way onto other albums. Terrific work by a gifted songwriter-storyteller.

S·E·L·E·C·T·E·D R·E·C·O·R·D·I·N·G·S

Peter Bellamy
(GREEN LINNET SIF 1001)
•
Peter Bellamy Sings the Barrack-Room Ballads of Rudyard Kipling
(GREEN LINNET SIF 1002)
•
Both Sides Then
(TOPIC 12TS400)
•
The Transports
(FREE REED FRRD 021/022)

Collectively, these four albums present a pretty good picture of what Peter Bellamy is all about. *Peter Bellamy* is a generous anthology of mainly traditional songs; the Kipling album shows some of his work putting the poet's words to music. *Both Sides Then* is something of a curiosity, as it contains music from both sides of the Atlantic, British and American, but it is an exciting record, and Bellamy is joined on it by such luminaries as Louis Killen, Dave Swarbrick, the Watersons, and his old Young Tradition sidekicks, Heather Wood and Royston Wood. *The Transports* is out of print, but first-rate performances from some of the leading figures of the folk scene, make it a masterpiece. Buy it, if you can find it.

Nic Jones
Nic Jones has been one of the leading lights of the English folk revival for many years, an enormously popular and

greatly respected figure known for a repertoire of interesting songs presented in interesting ways.

To anyone familiar with Jones's music, it will come as no surprise that Jones has cited Martin Carthy as a primary influence on his music. Like Carthy's, Jones's guitar tends to be percussive, with the bass carrying the melody line. But Jones's overall approach is more restrained than Carthy's, and his vocal style, while betraying some of Carthy's inflections, tends to be somewhat more ornamented. More recently, he has incorporated increased embellishment into his guitar playing, adding more pronounced counterpoint to the melody line, reflecting, perhaps, greater confidence in what was already fine playing.

The earlier influences on Jones's music are perhaps less apparent. Out of an interest in rock and roll, then in jazz guitarists, was born his interest in music. He was drawn to traditional music through the American folk revival and listened to Bert Jansch and Davey Graham as well as Chet Atkins. From all these people Jones assimilated various elements but developed a style all his own.

Jones is best known as a solo performer, but before he first struck out on his own, he was a member of a group called Halliard. After soloing for a while, Jones joined with Tony Rose and Pete and Chris Coe to form an acoustic group called Bandoggs. Bandoggs performed only occasionally, mainly because all its members were pursuing solo careers at the same time, but it added new dimensions to Jones's work because he was able to do things musically that he'd been unable to do on his own.

Jones has made five albums and guested on countless others, but they're likely to be all for a while at least. In 1982 he was critically injured in an automobile accident, and his recovery has been slow. Through his past achievements, he continues to be an important force in traditional music.

S·E·L·E·C·T·E·D R·E·C·O·R·D·I·N·G·S

The Noah's Ark Trap
(TRAILER LER 2091; SHANACHIE 79003)
·
Penguin Eggs
(TOPIC 12TS411)

When *The Noah's Ark Trap* was released, it was quickly hailed as the definitive Nic Jones LP, and there was idle speculation that there could be little room for improvement. With *Penguin Eggs*, however, he really outdid himself, and these albums together clearly represent his best work on record. *The Noah's Ark Trap* is a collection of traditional songs joined together without any breaks between cuts. On *Penguin Eggs* the material likewise is traditional (with one or two exceptions) and is characterized by flawless selections and superb arrangements. Truly essential.

Vin Garbutt

Unless you are a native of Tees-side, in northeastern England, chances are you may not be able to understand what Vin

Garbutt is singing. But even his overpowering dialect cannot mask the sheer energy of his music.

Like much of the music of the region, Garbutt's incorporates a characteristic bounciness with Celtic influences, augmented, no doubt, by the fact of Garbutt's own Irish heritage. He is an accomplished tin whistle player, but it is his singing that really makes people stand up and take notice. Garbutt is, not surprisingly, one of Britain's most popular singers, and one of the most exciting. He doesn't sing so much as he thrusts the sound out of his lungs, accompanied primarily by guitar. In live performances he combines his fervid style of singing with outrageous patter between numbers, making him something of a comedian as well. His singing is more decorated than that of many English singers, and he is gifted with a rich natural vibrato; he also seems to favor syncopation, as his music is often highly rhythmic.

Garbutt is a songwriter as well as an interpreter of traditional material. Most of his own compositions tend to confront contemporary issues, and recently he has generated considerable controversy because, a devout Catholic, he has taken an agressive Right-to-Life stance, which has antagonized and alienated many of his fans.

Political considerations aside, however, Garbutt is a highly individual and engaging performer whose music is a potent tool for reaching a wide audience.

S·E·L·E·C·T·E·D R·E·C·O·R·D·I·N·G·S

Eston California
(TOPIC 12TS378)
•
Tossin' a Wobbler
(TOPIC 12TS385)

These two albums are fairly similar, with a delightful combination of Garbutt's singing and whistle playing, but if you have to choose just one, go for *Tossin' a Wobbler*. Contemporary songs are better represented there, and the album notes convey a little of Garbutt's particular brand of humor. Either album makes for dynamic listening, however, and you're apt to find yourself wearing them out.

Shirley Collins

Although her music is firmly rooted in tradition, Shirley Collins has always been open to musical experimentation. And that, combined with her beautiful singing, is one of the major reasons she has been, and continues to be, a leading figure in the English folk revival.

A native of Sussex, Collins first came to national attention in the mid-1950s, when she recorded a song for Peter Kennedy on the program *Folksong Today*. She went on to assist Kennedy, Alan Lomax and Seamus Ennis in their collection of songs for the BBC, and she also helped with Lomax's *Folk Songs of North America* and *The Folk Songs of Britain* field recordings. She even accompanied Lomax on an extended field trip to the U.S., including a tour through the rural South.

In 1964 she joined guitarist Davey Graham in a legendary experiment, *Folk Roots, New Routes*, an album that combined

Graham's unique fusion of jazz, blues, Indian, and folk music with Collins's gentle, traditional singing style. It took amazing sophistication for both parties to realize that the harmonies of jazz and Indian music were compatible with English traditional ballads, and unfortunately the concept was so far ahead of its time that the album retreated into obscurity.

In 1967 Shirley's album *The Sweet Primeroses* was released, marking the debut of her sister Dolly's arrangements. Dolly, who is a classically trained musician and highly conversant with folk music, added a portative pipe organ, or flute-organ, to her sister's singing. The portable keyboard instrument is characterized by a hollow, pristine sound, something like several recorders all played together, and produced a splendid blend with Shirley's slightly breathy voice.

Other albums included collaborations with Mike Heron and Robin Williamson of the Incredible String Band and, in 1968, with the late David Munrow of the Early Music Consort. The latter, called *Anthems in Eden,* was the first folk "concept" album. It was a suite of traditional songs arranged by Dolly and linked with original instrumental compositions. The suite included the now classic "Dancing at Whitsun," written by Shirley's then husband Austin John Marshall and set to a traditional melody, and featured accompaniment on early musical instruments, played by members of Munrow's orchestra.

Shirley's marriage to Ashley Hutchings brought her into the electric folk arena. In 1971 Hutchings masterminded an album with Shirley singing to the amplified accompaniment of a group that was christened the Albion Band. The Albion Band went on to achieve considerable notoriety (sans Collins), but she participated in Hutching's first *Morris On* album before abandoning electric accompaniment.

Collins has never been terribly prolific, but her more recent albums have marked a return to the more conventional arrangements of *The Sweet Primeroses.* Another collaboration with Dolly has proved that the sisters have succeeded in an approach to traditional music that is at once accessible and yet retains the integrity of the tradition from which it stems.

S·E·L·E·C·T·E·D R·E·C·O·R·D·I·N·G·S

The Sweet Primeroses
(TOPIC 12T170)
•
Amaranth
(HARVEST SHSM 2008)
•
With the Albion Country Band:
No Roses
(CREST II United Kingdom)
•
With Davey Graham:
Folk Roots, New Routes
(RIGHTEOUS RECORDS GDC 001)

The Sweet Primeroses features Collins's singing with accompaniments by her sister Dolly on the marvelous portative pipe organ and other keyboard instruments. *Amaranth* is worth having for the *Anthems in Eden* suite, which fills side 2. Side 1 is a collection of traditional songs with electric accompaniment, and despite the inclusion of such musicians as Christopher Hogwood of the Early Music Consort, Collins's folk-rock period is better represented by _No Roses,_ an excellent album that hangs together well and offers first-rate supporting musicians.

You'll have to keep reminding yourself that _Folk Roots, New Routes_ was originally released in 1965. So far ahead of its time, the record is very much in step with today and reveals why the Collins/Graham collaboration was legendary.

Frankie Armstrong

You couldn't call Frankie Armstrong's singing pretty, but she is one of the most dynamic singers of the British folk revival. Singing largely unaccompanied, Armstrong touches on everything from the grand ballads to contemporary songs of social significance.

Regardless of whether her material is traditional or contemporary, however, she selects songs that speak to universal issues and concerns, from the violence and rape in the traditional "Prince Heathen" to the tragedy of drug addiction chronicled in the contemporary "Jack the Lad." Among her favorite songs are those voicing the concerns of women, whether it's the wenches who outwit the randy blades of the Child ballads or the cynical housewives of Leon Rosselson's songs. Undoubtedly, her preferences can be partly explained by the fact that she is an experienced social worker and has worked extensively with drug addicts and the blind.

Armstrong began singing in the late 1950s, drawn at first to the American folk music of the period. Eventually, however, she met up with some of the leading figures of the British revival, such as A.L. Lloyd and Ewan MacColl, and began singing British songs. There were few role models for her in those days; she has cited only Shirley Collins and Scottish singers Lucy Stewart, Jeannie Robertson, and Ray Fisher. Among the major influences on her was Louis Killen, with whom she traveled and sang for a while, and who urged her to develop the hardness in her voice that today is her trademark.

For as distinctive as the material she chooses to sing is Armstrong's unique style of singing. She has a remarkably powerful voice, tending to be rather deep and hard; at times it is almost strident, particularly when she sings ballads. She does include songs that lend themselves to a softer delivery, and sings them accordingly, but she doesn't have the subtle modulations that a singer like June Tabor does.

Frankie Armstrong isn't going to be everyone's cup of tea, but few can match her conviction and forcefulness. And it is when she is at her most powerful that she is at her best.

S·E·L·E·C·T·E·D R·E·C·O·R·D·I·N·G·S

Lovely on the Water
(TOPIC 12TS216)
•
Frankie Armstrong
(TOPIC 12TS273; ANTILLES AN-7021)

Lovely on the Water is a collection exclusively of tradi-
ional songs and probably Armstrong's best, although it
reflects fewer of her social concerns than her later
albums do. On *Frankie Armstrong* she added a couple of
contemporary songs, presaging the direction she since
taken in her career, and the social message is clear.

June Tabor

Anyone who's heard June Tabor sing isn't apt to forget the
experience. Endowed with a rich, expressive contralto, she
carries her singing a step further by applying intelligent,
sensitive interpretations of her material, and the effect is
powerful, at times even shattering.

Tabor began singing traditional music in her teens, when a
friend took her to a folk club and signed her up as a floor
singer. She quickly discovered the singing of Anne Briggs and
Belle Stewart, learned material off their records and became
captivated by their highly ornamented style of singing, which
she soon learned to emulate.

In college at Oxford, she encountered a large folk community, including a singer whose simpler style of singing began
to appeal to her. She started to use ornamentation more
sparingly, moving in the direction of the exquisite, controlled
singing that today is her trademark.

Early in her musical career, her repertoire was virtually all
unaccompanied, a characteristic that undoubtedly limited her
appeal, since many people find it difficult to listen to an entire
evening of solo unaccompanied song. What probably first
brought her wider acceptance and acclaim was her collaboration with Steeleye Span singer Maddy Prior on an album
called *Silly Sisters*. Later solo LPs likewise received raves, and
although these albums included a tasteful selection of traditional songs, presented unaccompanied as well as with guitar,
fiddle, bassoon, and synthesizer, perhaps most notable were
the songs she included by songwriter Eric Bogle. Both "And
the Band Played Waltzing Matilda" and "No Man's Land" are
now standards of the folk scene, and Tabor not only is in large
part responsible for exposing them to a wider audience, but
her versions of the songs remain possibly the best that have
ever been recorded.

More recently, Tabor has teamed up with guitarist Martin
Simpson. As a result her repertoire has broadened, including
a few songs by contemporary songwriters like Bill Caddick
and Richard Thompson, along with the ballads for which she
is known. She has also been influenced by Simpson's interest
in American music and has begun to sing such songs well.

S·E·L·E·C·T·E·D R·E·C·O·R·D·I·N·G·S

Airs and Graces
(TOPIC 12TS298)
•
Ashes and Diamonds
(TOPIC 12TS360)
•
With Martin Simpson:
A Cut Above
(TOPIC 12TS410)
•

With Maddy Prior:
Silly Sisters
(CHRYSALIS CHR1101; TAKOMA 7086)

All of these albums are excellent, but *A Cut Above* really is a cut above the others, marked by Tabor's singing at its best and Simpson's imaginative and ever-appropriate accompaniments. *Airs and Graces* met with high praise when it first appeared, and it remains many people's favorite, but reflects more of a purist approach to the material than either of Tabor's later LPs. *Ashes and Diamonds* was criticized in some quarters for being more commercial; accompaniments include synthesizer and electric guitar. But generally the songs are more accessible than on *Airs and Graces*. The high point of the record is Eric Bogle's "No Man's Land"—Tabor's is quite possible the best version of the song ever recorded. Tabor has also turned in first-rate performances on her inspired collaboration with Maddy Prior, *Silly Sisters*, which includes many lighthearted and beautiful songs.

Instrumentalists

There are many fine instrumentalists in the folk revival. Many, like John Kirkpatrick and Sue Harris, are nearly as well known as singers as for their instrumental work. Others, like Alistair Anderson, have been known to sing, but their instrumental work overshadows everything else they do.

Perhaps the major characteristic of the revival instrumentalists has been their willingness to experiment. Although the best are all well grounded in traditional and, in some cases, classical music, the best known have all strayed into other areas. Dave Swarbrick, for example, long a fixture on the folk scene, gained notoriety as the fiddle player for Fairport Convention.

Most instrumentalists work regularly with bands or do studio work, but Alistair Anderson and Dave Swarbrick both have earned well-deserved reputations independently as well.

Alistair Anderson

The ranks of concertina players are increasing all the time, but Alistair Anderson is in a class by himself. Long a member of the Northumbrian band the High Level Ranters, Anderson is as well known for his solo pursuits as he is for his now-ended stint with the Ranters.

Anderson traces his interest in traditional music back through the Rolling Stones to the bluesmen and Bob Dylan. A school friend gave him his first concertina, which he began playing despite the death of accomplished players on the instrument. A field trip to visit the great Northumbrian piper Billy Pigg, however, proved a turning point for Anderson in his approach to the concertina. More than anything, he was struck by the joy that Pigg took in his music, as well as by the staccato sound of the individual notes inherent in the dance tunes that the old man played. Unconsciously, he says, he began to emulate Pigg. At the age of 17, Anderson was asked to join the High Level Ranters.

Steeped in traditional music, Anderson nonetheless excels as a composer as well, creating tunes and arrangements that are fresh while at the same time compatible with traditional music. His concertina style is marked by fluidity and intricacy, on an instrument that too often is played in an oversimplified or overly staccato manner. His arrangements are deceptively simple at times, but always reflecting a sophisticated approach to music and harmony, and he is able to invoke music ranging from plaintive to exuberant. In concert Anderson often dances as he plays.

Yet Anderson's talents by no means end with the concertina. He is an accomplished piper as well, playing the Northumbrian smallpipes in the same precise, fluid style that characterizes his concertina playing.

Alistair Anderson's music is born of an innate pride in his Northumbrian homeland. And although he plays music from other traditions, it is as an ambassador of Northumbria that he concentrates his efforts, and a role at which he succeeds admirably.

S·E·L·E·C·T·E·D R·E·C·O·R·D·I·N·G·S

Traditional Tunes
(FRONT HALL FHR-08)
•
Steel Skies
(TOPIC 12TS427)

Traditional Tunes showcases Anderson's skill on both concertina and pipes, but it is marred by rather lackluster accompaniments on piano, guitar, and hammered dulcimer and winds up sounding like a parlor recital. *Steel Skies*, however, is vibrant, a delight from start to finish. Although rooted in tradition, all the tunes are Anderson originals and reveal him to be an excellent composer as well as instrumentalist.

Dave Swarbrick

Dave Swarbrick has been a mainstay of the British folk scene for so long, there's scarcely been a development in which he hasn't taken part. Swarbrick first came to attention as a member of Scotsman Ian Campbell's group, and his notoriety grew during the 1960s, when he and Martin Carthy played and recorded together in what proved a highly successful pairing. Best known for his superb fiddle playing, Swarbrick is an accomplished mandolin player as well.

Swarbrick's name can be found associated with such early ventures as the radio ballads and a number of early Topic LPs before he teamed up with Carthy. Late in the 1960s he joined Fairport Convention, bringing to the rock group an added emphasis on traditional music. He guested on the group's third album, but was a full-fledged member by the band's fourth effort, the ground-breaking *Liege and Lief*. He may not have been the most flamboyant member, but his influence was immediate and undeniable: his entry marked Fairport's whole-hearted foray into folk-rock, and his lively fiddling was equally effective whether accompanying singing or taking the lead in contemporary-flavored breaks. After joining the group, he found himself singing and writing songs, neither of which he had planned to do.

Swarbrick saw many changes in personnel during his lengthy stint with Fairport, yet always persisted as an influential figure on his own. While becoming the group's acknowledged leader, he guested on many albums by other folk artists, and when ear trouble forced him to concentrate once again on acoustic music, he slipped easily back into the folk milieu, even while retaining the electric aesthetic.

Few fiddle players anywhere in the world can match Swarbrick's sensitivity to his material, whether he's playing rock music or accompanying solo singing. His fiddle style is very distinctive, marked above all by liveliness, plus a penchant for subtle counterpoint to the melody and occasional, perfectly placed, embellishments. His mandolin playing is not quite as flamboyant as his fiddling but reflects many of the same qualities.

S·E·L·E·C·T·E·D R·E·C·O·R·D·I·N·G

Smiddyburn
(LOGO 1029)

This album harkens back to Swarbrick's days with Fairport, in that it is dominated by electric accompaniment and includes four of the band's former members. The material, is mostly traditional and very exciting.

Guitarists

Britain can boast some of the finest guitarists in the world; yet ironically, most of their early influences were American.

The skiffle movement and the folk revival were in full swing during the 1950s, and the guitar's popularity was at an all-time high, but most fledgling guitarists were merely imitating the simple-minded strumming that characterized skiffle. They heard an entirely different approach, however, when the American Ramblin' Jack Elliott visited England during the middle of the decade, for Elliott produced a sound infinitely more complex than anything that was being played in England at the time. The style took England by storm, and a whole new school of guitarists appeared, most of whom played watered-down blues and ragtime numbers.

When Davey Graham hit the scene in the early 1960s, his playing carried the possibilities of fingerpicking several steps further. Graham not only called upon blues, jazz and Indian influences; he combined them with traditional British music. His style was revolutionary, and had enormous influence on many young guitarists, including Bert Jansch and John Renbourn, whose playing today still reflects Graham's.

Revival singer Martin Carthy, however, came to develop an entirely new guitar style, one uniquely suited to traditional British music. To set off the modal melodies of British folk music, his style is marked by a drone, while he plays the melody on the bass strings. His technique is highly percussive, and the overall effect is remarkably powerful. Perhaps predictably, Carthy's approach has been widely imitated.

Not all guitarists in Britain have severed their ties with American guitar styles; John James is an excellent ragtime guitarist, and Martin Simpson has been working on a set of American Civil War tunes. Generally those guitarists who prefer black American music, however, play it in a gentler, more refined way than the bluesmen or ragtime originators did, and the most exciting guitar playing in Britain remains that which reflects uniquely British sensibilities.

S·E·L·E·C·T·E·D R·E·C·O·R·D·I·N·G

Fylde Acoustic
(TRAILER LER 2105)

This album, produced to promote the Fylde line of guitars in Britain, includes tracks by many acoustic guitarists of note in Britain and presents a valuable cross-section of styles. Very enjoyable and highly recommended.

Bert Jansch

If Davey Graham was the catalyst behind the so-called "folk baroque" style, Bert Jansch was its popularizer. As early as the 1960s, Jansch had a large following; he was living in London, playing a freewheeling blend of jazz-tinged contrapuntal accompaniments to songs ranging from original compositions to traditional ballads and an occasional blues number.

A native of Scotland, Jansch originally was exposed to folk music through the influence of Americans like Woody Guthrie and Bill Broonzy, whose music was being played at a local folk club. He took guitar lessons from Davey Graham's sister and from Archie Fisher at the club, but when both left, he found himself, as the most advanced student, teaching the rest of the students.

In time, Jansch made his way to London, where he was exposed to the British folk revival. In particular he was influenced by Anne Briggs, from whom he learned "Jack Orion" and several other traditional songs. Through her influence, and that of Davey Graham, he began experimenting with jazz-oriented accompaniments to traditional material. He also began writing, and his early topical song "Needle of Death" earned him widespread acclaim.

In the later 1960s, Jansch met John Renbourn, and the two became roommates. As might be expected of two musicians with a similar bent, they shared their music as well as their quarters, and the result was an album called *Bert and John,* a recording of largely original music with a jazz flavor.

In 1967 Jansch and Renbourn joined with drummer Terry Cox, bass player Danny Thompson, and singer Jacquie McShee to form the group Pentangle. Pentangle, which played amplified acoustic music, was the first group to play folk-influenced material and win international acclaim. After the group split up, Jansch went into semi-retirement, emerging in 1974 to record a new album.

Since then, he has made several albums with his group Conundrum, which includes Martin Jenkins on fiddle and

PHOTO BY SARAH LIFTON

Best known for intricate and often percussive finger-style playing, Bert Jansch has had a great influence upon a generation of British guitarists.

mandocello and Nigel Portman-Smith on bass. Like Pentangle, the group plays partly amplified acoustic music, some original and some traditional, but Jansch has continued to develop musically, and Conundrum's sound is more contemporary than Jansch's earlier efforts now seem.

Jansch's guitar style itself is a series of contradictions. He owes a clear debt to Graham, but he has carried the rudiments of Graham's style several steps further. His arrangements are intricate, but his touch is strong, frequently heavy and percussive, an element that developed not, as one might think, from the influence of American blues, but rather as a result of his attempts to play over the noise in crowded bars.

He doesn't shy away from syncopation, and throughout his career he has applied it to musical forms not conventionally associated with it.

Someone, unkindly, once described Jansch's singing as "the sound of dirty water disappearing down a plug-hole," but while his voice admittedly is not his primary strength, it has a gentle roughness that suits his music very well.

S·E·L·E·C·T·E·D R·E·C·O·R·D·I·N·G·S

Early Bert, Volume 2
(XTRA 1164)
•
Avocet
(CHARISMA CLASS 6; KICKING MULE KM 310)

Early Bert, Volume 2, originally released as *Jack Orion* around 1966, shows the folkier side of Jansch's playing and includes his excellent version of the song "Jack Orion." *Avocet* emphasizes original instrumentals and is strongly jazz tinged, but it is as notable for Martin Jenkins's contribution as for Jansch's.

John Renbourn

Of all the guitarists influenced by Davey Graham in the 1960s, none has come to have the breadth or the impact of John Renbourn. From his early collaborations with Bert Jansch, through Pentangle, up to the present and his collaboration with Stefan Grossman and his work with his own band, he has developed a dazzling guitar style characterized by refinement and vitality.

Musicianship the caliber of Renbourn's isn't born overnight, of course, and he has been at it for a long time. He acquired his first guitar at the age of 13, and went on to play in skiffle bands. Somewhere along the way he had two years of classical training, but it wasn't until Ramblin' Jack Elliott and Derroll Adams came to Britain that Renbourn learned to fingerpick. Like many British guitarists at the time, he initially played blues with a British accent—the basic tunes of the blues songs, but lacking the power of the black American bluesmen who originated them. In time, however, Renbourn heard both Bert Jansch and Davey Graham play and was intrigued by the fact that the music each was playing was altogether different from anything anyone else was playing. He quickly moved to emulate them—by his own admission, he used to copy everything from Graham—and around 1964 he and Jansch began playing together.

In 1967 Renbourn and Jansch founded Pentangle. Performing with the group consumed much of Renbourn's time, but he still managed to release three solo albums during the late 1960s and early 1970s, when the band was active.

After the breakup of Pentangle, Renbourn pretty much retired from the public eye for a while. He pursued an interest in early music, which had struck his fancy as early as his school days, and developed accompaniments based on counter-melodies, which he feels are suited to the modal melodies of traditional music. His interest in early music also led him to expand the open tunings he was already using, in

COURTESY OF THE RICHMOND ORGANIZATION

Flawless technique and impeccable taste have made the music of John Renbourn unparalleled for sophistication and refinement.

order to achieve effects that were impossible in standard tunings.

Renbourn finally emerged from his semi-retirement to record a couple of albums. He assembled a band with Jacquie McShee (called the John Renbourn Group) and continued the musical direction that Pentangle had been pursuing at the time of its breakup. Around the same time he recorded a remarkable album of solo guitar pieces, *The Hermit*. Not long afterward, Stefan Grossman approached Renbourn with the idea of collaborating on some tunes. The result was two albums of largely original contemporary compositions.

Renbourn's guitar style is characterized by a sure but delicate touch and a lyrical, fluid approach. His arrangements are at times astonishingly intricate, even when accompanying his singing. Although his interest in early music still seems to predominate, jazz, blues, ragtime, and Middle Eastern music all have played a role in shaping his style.

Renbourn's original compositions tend to be more contemporary in flavor. Most of these, he claims, are amalgams of tunes and riffs that he simply pieces together, although the finished product is clearly a coherent whole.

That Renbourn is a superb guitarist can scarcely be questioned. But perhaps more significant, he is a superb musician. For if a musician is someone who is remarkably sensitive to music, and who has the technical skill to express himself musically, then among guitarists, John Renbourn is in a class by himself.

S·E·L·E·C·T·E·D R·E·C·O·R·D·I·N·G·S

The Hermit
(TRANSATLANTIC TRA 336)
•

With the John Renbourn Group:
A Maid in Bedlam
(TRANSATLANTIC TRA 348; SHANACHIE 79004)

Both of these albums are sheer pleasure. *The Hermit* is devoted to solo guitar pieces, most remarkably complicated, and all flawlessly executed; the emphasis is on early music and traditional music. *A Maid in Bedlam* is the John Renbourn Group's first LP, and although the personnel have changed somewhat since it was released (with John Molineux replacing Sue Draheim), it nonetheless is a close approximation of the band's current sound and a work of art to boot. Renbourn's collaborations with Bert Jansch and Stefan Grossman and his work with Pentangle represent other aspects of his music.

Banding Together

It was perhaps inevitable that the wealth of first-rate musicians on the folk scene would begin to form into bands and duos. Not only was there the American example—the Weavers and the Kingston Trio—and skiffle, from the 1950s (however dismal the results), but musicians have always sought out other musicians for informal "sessions," and as the ranks of the folk revival grew and the level of musicianship improved, the opportunity developed for playing new, exciting music together in bands.

There is a tendency to think of British folk bands only in terms of the electric groups that dominated the scene during the 1970s—Pentangle, Fairport Convention, Steeleye Span, and so on. But in fact, all along there have been a significant number of groups, playing music from dance tunes to ballads sung unaccompanied and in harmony. Folk-rock currently has faded almost into oblivion, and in its place has developed a tremendous interest in country dance music. There remain many active groups of almost every persuasion on the scene, however, virtually guaranteeing something to fit every taste.

The Watersons

The Watersons are a family of singers from Yorkshire who have been, and continue to be, one of the most esteemed and influential groups on the folk scene. Originally composed of Mike, Lal, and Norma Waterson, plus their second cousin John Harrison, the group disbanded in the late 1960s, when Harrison moved to London, but re-formed in 1973, with Martin Carthy (Norma's husband) taking Harrison's place.

Although the Watersons have inevitably been compared with the Copper Family, who likewise are a family singing unaccompanied and in parts, in fact their sound is quite different. The Watersons don't sing in harmony so much as they sing parallel melodies, sometimes all singing the same tune, sometimes splitting up to sing different parts, then converging again. The overall effect is looser than the Coppers', with a certain amount of dissonance, and few groups of singers anywhere in the world can match their energy and excitement. Their repertoire is steeped in tradition, yet they have also been known to sing a stage song or two, and have recorded an entire album of sacred music.

The Watersons' singing style isn't highly ornamented, but it is marked by the "bleating" sound that characterizes many traditional singers. And while they may not all have beautiful voices in the classical sense, they are among the finest singers in Britain. Never overly polished, they reach their audiences on an emotional level; it is their rough edges and their rousing delivery that make their music so compelling.

S·E·L·E·C·T·E·D R·E·C·O·R·D·I·N·G·S

A Yorkshire Garland
(TOPIC 12TS167)
•
For Pence And Spicy Ale
(TOPIC 12TS265)
•
Green Fields
(TOPIC 12TS415)

It's hard to go wrong with anything the Watersons have recorded, and the selection is far greater than the albums listed here, but these three are certainly among the best. *A Yorkshire Garland,* recorded when John Harrison was still a member of the group, is an anthology of Yorkshire versions of familiar and not-so-familiar traditional songs. More than their first two albums, it is marked by boundless energy and, as usual, exceptional singing. *For Pence and Spicy Ale* was named the *Melody Maker* Folk Record of 1975 and was the first album produced by the re-formed group with Martin Carthy. The rousing rendition of "Country Life" alone is worth the price of the record, but the entire album is not to be missed. *Green Fields* is a collection of songs specifically about rural life and as such contains more than its share of truly beautiful songs, with the group's harmonies sounding better than ever. All the albums are fitted with copious notes by A. L. Lloyd.

High Level Ranters

Northumbria has long been an area rich in traditional music. Born of the region's isolation, the border wars with Scotland, and industry, which came to play so major a role in its economy and way of life, the music has a distinct style, characterized by a bounciness usually associated with Celtic strains.

For many years, the leading Northumbrian band has been the High Level Ranters. Although the lineup has changed recently, the group will probably always be best known for Tom Gilfellon on guitar and cittern, Alistair Anderson on concertina and Northumbrian smallpipes, Johnny Handle on accordion and keyboards, and Colin Ross on fiddle, whistle and pipes. All four sing as well, although Tom Gilfellon and Johnny Handle stand out as vocalists.

The Ranters have always attempted to keep their repertoire fresh, searching through old tune books and early printed folk song collections for new material. The group's sound is dominated by the free reed instruments in its lineup, concertina and accordion, but all the instruments blend effectively, creating a distinctive—and distinctively Northumbrian—music.

Although the High Level Ranters play both songs and dance tunes, in large doses, their music can start to sound monotonous. In 1981 the group lost both Alistair Anderson and Tom Gilfellon, and even though the High Level Ranters have continued to record, with Jim Hall and Peter Wood now in the lineup, the band's earlier efforts remain its best.

S·E·L·E·C·T·E·D   R·E·C·O·R·D·I·N·G

Ranting Lads
(TOPIC 12TS297)

The High Level Ranters have produced many albums, all pretty good, all fairly similar. This one is typical, with a pleasing blend of songs and tunes. Tom Gilfellon's singing is excellent, as always, as is Johnny Handle's. Alistair Anderson's instrumental work is also worthy of note.

John Kirkpatrick and Sue Harris

Individually and collectively, John Kirkpatrick and Sue Harris are perhaps best known as instrumentalists—Kirkpatrick as a virtuoso on almost any free reed instrument and Harris on oboe and hammered dulcimer—yet each is a first-rate singer as well, and they have appeared in both capacities on many albums in addition to recording several of their own.

Kirkpatrick, in fact, first came to traditional music through singing. As a member of several choral groups, including a choir at a church in Hammersmith, which started holding country dances, he became involved in the dance revival and was encouraged to learn to play the melodeon. In the following years Kirkpatrick played for country dances with several bands and became increasingly well known on the folk circuit. In 1970 he turned professional.

Shortly after, he met Sue Harris, who had just finished college and was trained as a music teacher. Although piano was her first instrument, she also played oboe, on the surface an unlikely candidate for traditional-style music but one that in Harris's hands seemed perfectly suited to folk music. In 1972 Harris quit her teaching position and joined Kirkpatrick full time.

Not long after turning professional, Kirkpatrick was asked to join Shirley Collins in a small tour of Devon. The tour with Collins led to his appearance on her *No Roses* album, and to his inclusion on what became a landmark album—*Morris On.*

As a result of his participation in these projects, Kirkpatrick was asked to join the first Albion Band, a request he turned down. Around the beginning of 1973, both he and Harris were persuaded to join the band and appeared on the album *Battle of the Field* before the group split up.

Kirkpatrick and Harris play in Umps and Dumps, one of the many country dance bands currently experiencing great popularity. And it was during the early stages of Umps and Dumps that Harris began playing hammered dulcimer, because she was pregnant and couldn't apply the physical pressure that playing the oboe required. She quickly became enamored of the instrument and highly proficient on it.

Some of Kirkpatrick's most interesting work involves Martin Carthy. They had played together in Steeleye Span for a brief time and enjoyed playing together, so Kirkpatrick joined Carthy on his albums *Because It's There* and *Out of the Cut* and both went on to form the country dance band Brass Monkeys.

Without exception, the music of John Kirkpatrick and Harris is characterized by a high level of technical skill, plus infectious energy. Their material runs to dance music more than songs, yet the fact that both are fine singers as well as instrumentalists means that their music never grows stale.

S·E·L·E·C·T·E·D R·E·C·O·R·D·I·N·G·S

Among the Many Attractions at the Show Will Be a Really High Class Band
(TOPIC 12TS295)
•
Facing the Music
(TOPIC 12TS408)

Unfortunately, many of the albums Kirkpatrick and Harris recorded were on the now-defunct Free Reed label, so their availability is precarious at best. These two, on Topic, however, are not only available, they are among their best. *Among the Many Attractions...* is an excellent collection of songs and tunes that points up the duo's versatility. *Facing the Music* is an instrumental album and includes a couple of American tunes along with the British ones. It is a spirited and joyful record.

The Electric Connection

Throughout the heyday of folk-rock, the key name has been Ashley Hutchings. A competent but not shining bass player, Hutchings has a genius for assembling people who are able to create outstanding music together. First a founding member of Fairport Convention, Hutchings went on to found Steeleye Span, then the various incarnations of the Albion Band. Save Pentangle, he has been at the forefront of virtually every development in electric folk music.

Pentangle had already been together for two years when Fairport Convention began to pursue folk music in earnest, and it's difficult to imagine that Pentangle's success didn't have some influence on Fairport's decision, but Fairport was basically a rock band, and the traditional material they played was little more than an experiment. Steeleye Span was an outgrowth of Fairport's foray into traditional music, and was oriented mainly toward folk. The Albion Band, however, adopted a somewhat different approach. Originally the group of musicians gathered to accompany Shirley Collins on her album *No Roses,* it pursued the direction Hutchings had begun to explore on his *Morris On* album, a record of Morris dance tunes and songs set to amplified accompaniment.

The electric folk movement hasn't so much died as run out of steam. Its acceptance in folk circles was always erratic at best, and the execution of the songs was often heavy-handed. And, too, once the music ceased being a novelty, it became clear that the songs and tunes really were better served through gentler treatment.

Pentangle:
The Pentangle
(REPRISE RS 6315)
•
Solomon's Seal
(REPRISE MS 2100)

Pentangle, which formed in 1967, was the first British group to achieve commercial success performing traditional music, and while they didn't play electric instruments, their use of amplified acoustic instruments forcast the folk-rock movement that soon followed. Their music was a true fusion of styles, combining jazz, folk, American, and Eastern influences, much as Jansch's and Renbourn's guitar styles did. The group's sound was dominated by Jacqui McShee's crystalline vocals and enhanced by Danny Thompson's inspired bass runs. You'll probably have to comb the used-record bins for these albums, and any others by Pentangle. *The Pentangle* is the band's first album, and a conglomeration of traditional, contemporary, and original material. *Solomon's Seal* will probably appeal more to folk fans, as the majority of the songs are traditional and very tastefully arranged.

Fairport Convention:
History of Fairport Convention
(ISLAND ICD 4)
•
Liege and Lief
(ISLAND ILPS 9115; A&M 4257)

Their lineup changed so often, they were dubbed "Fairport Confusion." But Fairport Convention was the first band to play folk-rock, and for a long time was a leading force in the folk-rock "movement." Their main assets were Sandy Denny, whose voice resembled Grace Slick's only without the stridency; Richard Thompson, guitarist and songwriter par excellence; and Dave Swarbrick, the wonderfully creative fiddle and mandolin player. *History of Fairport Convention,* a two-record set, tracks the development of the group's music over a decade. Many of their best numbers are here, from traditional ballads to Denny's and Thompson's original compositions. *Liege and Lief* is the group's definitive folk-rock album, and a record that has been highly influential. Folk fans would probably prefer it to the survey album.

Steeleye Span:
Please to See the King
(CREST 8)

•

Below the Salt
(CHRYSALIS 1008)

Whereas Fairport was basically a rock band that played traditional music, Steeleye members saw themselves as folk musicians who happened to play amplified instruments, and in its heyday Steeleye Span was blessed

Steeleye Span tastefully adapted electric instruments to the English ballad and country dance tradition.

COURTESY OF CHRYSALIS RECORDS, INC.

with a plethora of talent and energy, led by Tim Hart and Maddy Prior. The band continues to be a presence, if not a force, on the British folk scene, but its unstable lineup has included some of the foremost musicians in England. These two albums are generally acknowledged as the group's best efforts. *Please to See the King* includes Martin Carthy and founder Ashley Hutchings, whose contributions are everywhere in evidence. *Below the Salt* contains some of the most beautiful music the band ever made. Although both Carthy and Hutchings had left by the time it was recorded, the music has in no way suffered, and the entire record is a delight.

The Albion Band:
Morris On
(ISLAND IRSP 6)

•

Battle of the Field
(ANTILLES AN-7027)

The Albion Band actually isn't one group but several, all of which have been marked by Ashley Hutchings's guiding presence and an emphasis on English dance music. *Morris On* isn't actually an Albion album but a first cousin, and as you might expect, Morris dance tunes and songs predominate. It is a very upbeat record, with surprising variety for an album with so focused a subject. *Battle of the Field* places less emphasis on dance music than other Albion records, but contains some first-rate performances by John Kirkpatrick and Martin Carthy, who briefly were members of the group.

Dance Music

Ashley Hutchings clearly had his finger on the pulse of the folk revival. First pioneering the field of folk-rock, he went on to combine electric instrumentation with English dance music. And that has proved to be an area ripe for a revival of its own.

Not that dance music is anything new or had ever died away completely. For years Morris teams persisted as a quaint if puzzling anachronism, and there were bands all over England playing traditional dance music of other kinds, whether the Cheviot Ranters in the northeast or the musicians from the south that Topic recorded. Early manifestations of the trend tended to be localized, with dance bands merely providing the accompaniment for dances and ceilidhs. But the popularity of such events, and the music that went along with them, escalated, and dance bands playing southern English dance tunes—polkas, schottishes, jigs, and so on—proliferated. One early revival group was Oak, a four-piece band composed of Tony Engle, currently director of Topic Records; Rod Stradling on melodeon; Peta Webb on vocals and fiddle, and Danny Stradling on vocals and tambourine.

The dominant instruments in southern English dance music are melodeon and hammered dulcimer, which contribute to the lively rhythmic quality of the genre, and of all the groups that have sprung up, the leading band continues to be the Old Swan Band, most of whose members are multi-instrumentalists.

Unless you dance, however, you may find it difficult to get worked up over Old Swan or indeed any English country dance band. To the uninitiated, one band sounds pretty much like another, and one dance tune disconcertingly like the one that preceded it.

Still, there's no denying the popularity of the country dance bands, and maybe aficionados of the genre know something the rest of us don't. To be fair, the music isn't bad so much as merely boring. Most of the musicians involved in it, in fact, are of the highest caliber. But dance bands would do well to concentrate on playing for dances. Like most music, once removed from original context, it suffers in translation.

One optimistic note on the scene, however, is Brass Monkeys, the band Martin Carthy and John Kirkpatrick have put together. It promises to raise dance music out of the artistic doldrums.

S·E·L·E·C·T·E·D R·E·C·O·R·D·I·N·G·S

The Old Swan Band:
Gamesters, Pickpockets and Harlots
(DINGLES DIN 322)

In small doses, this is actually a very enjoyable album. But chances are, you won't want to play it through each time you listen to it because the tunes all start to run together. The album cover is wonderful.

Songwriters

Although folk-oriented songwriters by no means confine their efforts to political subject matter, contemporary folk songs have their origins in political causes of the 1950s and 1960s. Ewan MacColl, in particular, began writing songs as political tools, as early as the 1930s. Today, Leon Rosselson is carrying the ball, writing songs that reflect his social conscience.

The composed songs popular on the folk scene run the gamut from counterfeit traditional ballads to social and political commentary to obscure spiritual references. Some, like those of Ewan MacColl and Cyril Tawney, have been absorbed into the tradition, indicating that they are fulfilling the same needs in people's lives that the older, traditional songs did.

Leon Rosselson

If he had been active in America during the 1960s, chances are Leon Rosselson's name would be as well known today as Tom Paxton's, Phil Ochs's, or Tom Lehrer's. For Rosselson is a brilliant songwriter of biting satires and social and political commentary, usually with a leftist bent, and his use of language to make a point is, quite simply, remarkable.

Rosselson's musical roots go back to his university days, in the late 1950s, when the English folk revival was young and Rosselson was a member of a very popular group called the Galliards. "I started at the top," he once said, "and have been working my way downward since." Rosselson's music today appeals not to the mass audience but to people unafraid of thinking. And while he is not a folk singer, he usually finds his audience in the folk clubs.

Because Rosselson has a limited range vocally, he began writing songs when he started singing solo; he was forced to generate his own material to suit his voice. "Since I can deal with words, if not with tunes," he has said, "I wrote songs with lots of words and little tunes. I've tried to be aware of all the different things that have been happening around me to write songs about the way I look at those things."

As one might imagine, Rosselson is seldom at a loss for words, and his songs tend to be verbose, at times almost unwieldy, because there are barely enough beats for all the syllables he tries to cram in. Yet at his best, Rosselson succeeds at presenting highly unusual perspectives on commonly accepted situations. His song "Stand up for Judas," for example, which approaches the New Testament as a sociological study, concludes that Judas, not Jesus, had the best interests of the poor in mind. Occasionally almost surrealistic, his lyrics create exaggerated worlds tempered only by their commentary upon reality, much as the novels *1984* and *Brave New World* do. His songs reflect outrage, wistfulness, irony, and cynicism, usually with a current of humor running through them. And it's the humor and the cleverness that prevent his music from becoming heavy-handed, despite its wordy, didactic nature.

Rosselson frequently has collaborated with singer Roy Bailey, whose clear tenor is more appropriate than Rosselson's hard, ironic tone whenever the subject of a song calls for a more stirring delivery or a more sensitive approach. When performing in concert, Rosselson and Bailey work from scripts, developing programs around central themes and weaving the songs in around quotes from media relevant to the topic at hand. Unfortunately, the Rosselson-Bailey collaboration ended, all the more regrettable since Bailey played an active role in popularizing some of Rosselson's material.

S·E·L·E·C·T·E·D R·E·C·O·R·D·I·N·G·S

With Roy Bailey:
Love, Loneliness, Laundry
(FUSE CF 271)
•
If I Knew Who the Enemy Was
(FUSE CF 284)

Both these albums are excellent and show Rosselson's songs at their best. Credit is undoubtedly due Martin Carthy, who produced them and, along with Rosselson, arranged the material. Certainly Roy Bailey's singing plays a major role, too, as his voice is enough to send shivers down the spine. Of the two records, *Love, Loneliness, Laundry* is probably the best place to start, as it contains two of Rosselson's all-time best compositions—"Don't Get Married, Girls," a bitingly witty commentary on womanhood, and "Stand Up for Judas." The high point of *If I Knew . . .* ironically isn't a Rosselson song: "The Testimony of Patience Kershaw," which Bailey sings unaccompanied, was taken from the transcripts of a hearing held in the 19th century, investigating conditions in the mines, and it is a powerful statement about the effects of the Industrial Revolution.

Ralph McTell

It's hard to gauge what Ralph McTell's impact would have been if he'd never written "Streets of London." Until he wrote that hit song, he was just another English kid inspired by the skiffle movement and, later, by Ramblin' Jack Elliott, to pick up a guitar and do a Woody Guthrie act. But "Streets of London" almost literally pulled him off the streets of London—and Paris—where he had been playing for tips, and into the limelight as one of the most popular British songwriters.

PHOTO BY SARAH LIFTON

Songwriter Ralph McTell had a
popular hit with "Streets of London"
but continues to find his audience
among folk fans.

Actually, there can be some dispute over whether McTell can accurately be called a folk singer, since these days he sticks pretty much to his own material. But in the early days of his career, his repertoire was comprised of old Blind Blake rags, Woody Guthrie songs, and so on, and there was no place for him to play but the folk clubs. As he began writing more songs and incorporating them into his act, the clubs continued to book him, and he has remained associated with the folk scene, despite the fact that his most famous song made number 1 on the pop charts and has been recorded more than 50 times by other musicians and translated into several foreign languages.

McTell's original material is marked by eclecticism. His subjects have included everything from the street people of London to the obligatory love songs, a paean to Sylvia Plath, childhood memories, World War I, insanity, and drug abuse. Many of his songs are profoundly moving; others border on banality. Of all the major folk-oriented songwriters in Britain today, McTell's material has the strongest ties with mainstream popular music. But many folk fans find his songs both accessible and appealing.

Perhaps the key to understanding McTell's music lies in the fact that he views himself more as an entertainer than as an artist. He is, in fact, a superb live performer, as might be expected; yet his manner on stage is modest, if not self-effacing. His gentle, slightly nasal voice is pleasing, although sometimes one wishes it was a trifle more expressive; if it weren't for his songwriting, there would be little to distinguish him from countless other pleasant-voiced men with guitars.

Except for his guitar playing. McTell has retained his early interest in Blind Blake rags, which has lent his guitar style a flair and technical competence that isn't often matched among singer-songwriters. His ragtime playing lacks the verve of the original sources, but it has great spirit and, given his proficiency on the instrument, it isn't surprising that he says his guitar often dictates his songs to him; he usually comes up with the tune first, and it may be weeks before he adds words. More recently he has added piano accompaniment to some of his songs, although it's clear he could use more practice to bring it up to the level of his guitar playing.

McTell's music may be a little too commercial-sounding for the die-hard folk fan. But it frequently is sensitive, articulate, and affecting.

S·E·L·E·C·T·E·D R·E·C·O·R·D·I·N·G

Ralph McTell Live
(FANTASY F-9571)
•
Released in Britain as
Ralph, Albert and Sydney
(WARNER BROTHERS K-56399)

Ralph McTell has made many albums, but this one, his only live album, is head and shoulders above the others. Not only does it contain his best—and best-known—songs; it benefits from the simple guitar arrangements that characterize his concert performances. The songs themselves, along with McTell's engaging personality, are permitted to dominate, rather than the schmaltzy, intrusive arrangements that so often accompany his recorded efforts.

Richard Thompson

The fact that both folk and rock audiences embrace the music of Richard Thompson only points up the breadth of its appeal. For the ex-Fairport Conventioneer not only is a skillful guitarist, he is a songwriter of considerable depth, and one who is having a profound influence on contemporary music.

Although Thompson's music no longer can strictly be considered folk, it clearly owes a debt to more traditional sources. He himself has said that its roots are in Celtic music, as well as early rock and roll, Middle Eastern music, and various other musical genres that have appealed to him, but a Thompson discography is even more revealing. In addition to Fairport Convention, Thompson played on the first *Morris On* album, and has guested on a number of albums folkier than his own. Furthermore, some of his earlier compositions reveal a direct connection with traditional sources: "The New St. George" resembles Morris tunes in format if not lyrics, and "Wheely Down" is accompanied by a common traditional device—the drone. Then, too, the backup musicians who join him on his albums have impeccable folk credentials.

Thompson frequently takes traditional forms and twists them so that their source remains recognizable, but at the same time the result sounds unmistakably like contemporary rock. His music transcends any superficial impressions, however. Much of it is moody, deliberately obscure, conveying a bleakness even when the meaning of the song is not immediately apparent.

Thompson first gained notoriety as Fairport Convention's lead guitarist, and although he is best known for his electric lead work, he is an accomplished acoustic guitarist as well, with an intricate, clean style. On many of his albums he is joined by his now-estranged wife Linda, and until recently the duo had been an extraordinarily dynamic force on the folk scene. Linda's clear voice handles his material well, providing at times a welcome respite from Thompson's own distinctive but limited vocals.

It is Richard Thompson's songs, however, that are most apt to have lasting impact. Several, like "Down Where the Drunkards Roll" and "Strange Affair" have become virtual standards in the folk clubs, and increased media attention seems to forecast broader exposure and acceptance for Thompson's music.

S·E·L·E·C·T·E·D R·E·C·O·R·D·I·N·G·S

Henry the Human Fly
(ISLAND IRSP 20)
•
I Want to See the Bright Lights Tonight
(ISLAND ILPS 9266)
•
Shoot Out the Lights
(HANNIBAL RECORDS HNBL 1303)

Henry the Human Fly and *I Want to See the Bright Lights Tonight* both contain some of Thompson's best-known songs, all presented in Thompson's inimitable rock-oriented way. There's a quality of uneasiness to *Shoot Out the Lights,* underscored by the Thompsons' split after it was released. Yet here Thompson's songwriting comes into its own as it never did before, with consistently intelligent, evocative material throughout, and an assemblage of musicians that lends excitement to the arrangements.

SCOTLAND

The music of Scotland, like its culture, is the product of two distinct influences—the Celtic and the Anglo-Saxon. The Celtic has dominated the Highlands, where the Gaels settled as the Anglo-Saxons took over increasing amounts of farmland in the Lowlands; the Anglo influence has dominated the Lowlands. Each region has its own linguistic idiosyncrasies; Gaelic is still spoken in some places in the Highlands, while the Lowlands has its own unique dialect. By no means are the two strains entirely distinct, however. As is inevitable whenever cultures exist side by side over many years, there has been a great deal of exchange, and nowhere is this more apparent than in traditional Scottish music.

While the same kinds of influences that shaped England's folk music tradition have been at work in Scotland as well, at the same time Scotland's music has reflected its history in a far more visible way. The political conflicts between England and Scotland, for example, have manifested themselves over and over in the music. Many such songs document the Scottish uprisings against the English, such as the Jacobite rebellions of 1715 and 1745, or chronicle border skirmishes. Other songs confront social conditions.

Two distinctly Scottish forms of song both are related to work. Waulking songs were the result of communal labor, and were used to set the pace and rhythm as the women shrank newly woven cloth. Bothy ballads were the product of farm laborers who lived and worked under the bothy system. Conditions often were grim, and many bothy ballads focused on the hard life of the farm servant; others spoke of the farmer or his wife; still others celebrated different tasks that were performed and the workers who did them.

Scotland's history likewise has shaped her instrumental traditions. During the 18th century, for example, church and state attempted to suppress the bagpipes; as a result the fiddle gained in importance. When the ban against playing the bagpipes finally was lifted, the bagpipe was transformed from a solo instrument to part of a military bagpipe band.

Yet another formative factor in Scots traditional music has been the fact that much of it was written under patronage. Until the 16th century, Highland clan chiefs retained bards to write songs and poems for various occasions; they likewise supported pipers for similar reasons, up through the 18th century. Fiddlers, too, came to write for commissions, and many of the tunes that were composed both for fiddle and for pipes were written down and preserved.

The travelers, or gypsies, have been particularly influential in Scots music. These people, often the descendants of those displaced by the Highland clearances of the late 18th and early 19th centuries, had little contact with mainstream society until this century. Their main source of entertainment was their music, and such musicians as the ballad singer Jeannie Robertson were the products of their tradition.

As the result of social and geographical conditions, the distinction between art music and traditional music in Scotland has often been obscured, and traditional music has never really been in danger of dying out. Consequently, there has never been as much place for a folk music "revival" in Scotland as there has been in England. Yet the English revival added impetus to the tradition that already existed in Scotland and directed increasing numbers of people back to their own folk music. Probably the leading figure to play a major role this century in furthering Scottish traditional music has been Hamish Henderson of the School of Scottish Studies. Like the late A. L. Lloyd, Henderson is a renowned scholar and writer and a noted collector as well. Not only was he responsible for discovering Jeannie Robertson, but his research also led to the discovery of the Stewarts of Blairgowrie. Henderson likewise influenced the careers of many now-familiar revival singers, including Jean Redpath and Ray Fisher, and was involved in the BBC's folk music program during the 1950s. Henderson's skills extend to songwriting and poetry as well; best known among his songs are "The 51st Highland Division's Farewell to Sicily" and "Freedom Come All Ye." Presently the keeper of a large archive of folk song at the School of Scottish Studies, Henderson has contributed immeasurably to an awareness of the rich Scottish musical tradition.

The Highland Bagpipe

There is perhaps no other musical instrument more firmly linked with a country than the Highland bagpipe is with Scotland. And there is probably no other musical instrument that has been subject to both the veneration and the ridicule that the bagpipe has.

The Highland bagpipe is the best known of the family of reed instruments driven by a bag of air and characterized by a series of drones plus a chanter that carries the melody. Unlike its cousins, the Irish uilleann pipes and the English Northumbrian smallpipes, which are pumped by a bellows, the Highland bagpipe is mouth blown, which accounts for its louder, harsher tone, as the reeds must be harder to allow for the moisture.

Although popular opinion has it that historically the bagpipe was first and foremost a military instrument, this is only partly true. Originally used for playing dance tunes and slow airs, the bagpipe succeeded bardic poetry and the harp in their role in battle.

The bagpipe was an important instrument among the Highland clans, and the piper an honored member of a Highland chief's retinue. This position was largely the result of the MacCrimmon family, who were the hereditary pipers to the MacLeod clan from the 16th century until the late 18th century. The MacCrimmons revolutionized bagpipe music by developing the *piobaireachd*, or Great Music, which transformed the bagpipe from a rustic instrument used for airs and dances to a noble instrument with a musical form all its own. The *piobaireachd* was used to commemorate great people and events and is marked by the use of an air and variations, played slowly and with dignity. Pipers who played the Great Music scorned the lighter, or middle music—the slow airs and jigs. And the light music, which today comprises the majority of pipe tunes, has only become known in the last century or so.

The middle of the 18th century saw Highland piping in a crisis. With the defeat of the Jacobites in 1745, and the subsequent Disarming Act of 1747, the bagpipes, along with virtually all other manifestations of Scottish culture, were banned. The pipes had been declared a weapon within the context of battle and could only be played by special permit.

More devastating, however, was the fact that many Highland chiefs forfeited their land, rendering them unable to support their pipers anymore.

Happily, however, piping was being adapted to a new function. In 1757, William Pitt had raised regiments from among the Highlanders, and within the ranks of the first regiment were 30 pipers and drummers, who were permitted under law to play the pipes. Later regiments were similarly supplied with pipers. Around 1840 the idea of the military pipe band was born.

During the 19th century pipers continued to play a role in the military. Piping competitions, begun in 1781 by the Highland Society, also continued. And the legacy of the MacCrimmons was passed on through their many students and continues to this day.

John Burgess

Although increasingly today the bagpipe is used with other instruments, as in the Battlefield Band and the Tannahill

Weavers, it remains a solo instrument as well. Probably the finest living practitioner of Scottish piping is John Burgess. Burgess first expressed interest in the bagpipes at the age of 4, when his father made him a practice chanter. He began taking lessons at the age of 10, and first played professionally at the age of 16.

Burgess has been the recipient of many prizes for his piping and is now a piping teacher. He is a versatile musician, excelling at the Great Music as well as the middle music and light music. The latter, which includes marches, strathspeys, reels, and hornpipes, undoubtedly began as accompaniment to dances but has come to be the source of display pieces for pipers, and the digital pyrotechnics required for playing it has made it a popular part of any piper's repertoire.

S·E·L·E·C·T·E·D   R·E·C·O·R·D·I·N·G

The Art of the Highland Bagpipe, Volume 1
(TOPIC 12TS291)

It would be misleading to say that this record is easy to listen to. Unless you're an aficionado of bagpiping, the novelty is apt to wear off very quickly. Yet taken a little at a time, the intricacy of the music still dazzles, and Burgess's fluid playing reveals him to be a master of this most controversial of instruments.

Fiddle Music

As the Highland bagpipes were suffering something of a decline in the early 18th century, the fiddle was, in turn, coming to the fore in Scotland, and the 18th century proved to be the heyday of Scots fiddle music.

In 1745, the same year as the Jacobite defeat, Niel Gow won the Scottish national fiddle championship. Gow was an accomplished and influential performer, but he became best known as a composer. His music was performed by chamber groups featuring a variety of instruments, as well as on the fiddle alone. In time his son Nathaniel also became one of the leading fiddlers of his day, and the Gows' music has remained an important part of any Scottish fiddler's repertoire.

The Scots fiddle style owes a lot to the bagpipe. Many of the decorations commonly heard on the fiddle can be traced back to the ornamentation characteristic of piping. Perhaps the most readily identifiable element in Scottish fiddling is a unique triplet, known as the snap.

Because fiddle music consists primarily of dance tunes, it is no surprise that traditionally fiddling was heard primarily at large dances or balls. Jigs and reels were common dance tunes, but by far the most distinctive type was the strathspey. The strathspey is actually a slow reel and is unique to Scotland. Other fiddle tunes, the slow airs, were not used for dances but either composed for specific occasions or derived from songs.

J. Scott Skinner

One of the greatest of Scots fiddlers, J. Scott Skinner was born in 1843. Skinner learned fiddle technique from a variety of sources; his brother Sandy taught him the basics and he went on to pick up additional technique from Peter Milne and from French violinist Charles Rougier.

Although Skinner wanted to pursue the study of dance, like his father and brother, with the aim of becoming a dance teacher, he continued playing the fiddle. In 1863 he won a competition at Inverness and eventually abandoned his plans, to concentrate on the fiddle. He was best known in Britain—indeed, something of a celebrity—but he made two trips to the United States, in 1893 and in 1926. He was a pioneer recording artist and recorded cylinders for Edison and discs for Emile Berliner.

Skinner's repertoire paid tribute to the fiddling champions who had gone before him, but he was a prolific composer himself and the author of over 600 pieces for the fiddle. As a performer, Skinner was probably best known for his bowing technique; his style was lively and fluid, and the influence of the bagpipe is readily apparent in his playing.

The Strathspey King, as Skinner was dubbed, died in 1927. Yet even today his playing remains a standard for other fiddle players to strive toward.

S·E·L·E·C·T·E·D R·E·C·O·R·D·I·N·G

The Music of Scott Skinner
(TOPIC 12TS268)

Half this album is made up of recordings by Skinner himself, half of Skinner's music as played by Bill Hardie, considered to be the leading follower of Skinner alive today. The fidelity naturally suffers on Skinner's tracks—the earliest dates back to 1908—but even through the hissing and crackling it is clear why he was legendary. To piano accompaniment, he produces performances of enormous vitality. Hardie's contribution not only benefits from modern fidelity; it enables the listener to get a better idea of what Skinner's style was probably like, since the notes aren't muffled by surface noise. Ultimately, however, the master somehow comes through with more finesse and showmanship.

Shetland Fiddling

Although the Shetland Islands are part of Scotland, geographically they are slightly closer to Norway, so it should come as no surprise that their musical influences are derived as strongly from Scandinavia as from mainland Scotland.

Fiddle music predominates on Shetland, primarily because for many years the fiddle was the only instrument to be found there, the result, no doubt, of the islands' isolated location. Although Scots and Irish music has been very influential, the Hardanger fiddle tradition of Norway has also come to bear. The Hardanger fiddle has a series of strings that vibrate in sympathy to those being played and while the Shetland fiddlers play standard four-string violins, they often use tunings and techniques reminiscent of the Hardanger sound. The most audible of the Hardanger influences has been in the use of the drone, but the Norwegian tradition is also apparent in the tunes themselves, many of which are the same as the Norwegian ones and even bear Norwegian names.

Another characteristic of Shetland fiddling is a concern with the supernatural. Many of the traditional Shetland tunes are said to be those of the "trows," Shetland counterparts to the Scandinavian trolls. Traditionally, many fiddlers were reputed to have learned various tunes from the trows, whose music filtered up from their homes underground.

In time, returning seamen introduced other instruments to the Shetland Islands. Most notable among these were the guitar, banjo, and mandolin. Although the mandolin is still played to some extent, only the guitar really caught on and has endured, and fiddle music remains Shetland's main musical resource.

The two leading exponents of Shetland Islands fiddle music today are Tom Anderson and his ex-pupil Aly Bain. Anderson was taught to play the fiddle by his grandfather and has been a major promoter of traditional fiddle music in Shetland. He organized the Shetland Fiddlers Society and is the first teacher of traditional fiddle music in Shetland to be employed by the government. Anderson is well known from performances on radio and has made a number of records.

Aly Bain was Anderson's next-door neighbor and became interested in the instrument at an early age, the result of hearing Anderson play. He became one of Anderson's students, and in the early 1970s began playing in Boys of the Lough, a well-known multinational band playing the traditional music of Scotland, Ireland, and the Shetland Isles. Bain is justifiably considered one of the best fiddlers in Britain.

S·E·L·E·C·T·E·D R·E·C·O·R·D·I·N·G·S

The Silver Bow
(TOPIC 12TS281; PHILO 2019)
•
Shetland Folk Fiddling, Volume 2
(TOPIC 12TS379)

These are two similar albums of Shetland fiddling, with piano accompaniment, and some guitar added on Volume 2. Each features Tom Anderson, Aly Bain, and Anderson's students, playing both in unison and harmonizing. The second seems substantially more spirited than the first and is more highly recommended for that reason, but each represents the Shetland style and is of particular interest to anyone interested in fiddle music.

Source Singers

Scotland has been less dependent than England on isolated rural communities for the preservation of her musical traditions. Whether in the Scottish countryside or in the cities, the singing tradition has remained alive through the present, partly through the influence of the nomadic travelers.

The Scots singing style tends to be more dramatic and ornamented than the English, but less so than the Irish. Although traditional singing is basically unaccompanied, Scottish singers have developed vocal techniques that emulate various musical instruments, most notably the bagpipes. A distinctive element of the Scots tradition is the so-called mouth music, which is perhaps best described as an early version of scat singing. The syllables that comprise the sounds are sometimes nonsensical, but more often have meaning and are sung in a rapid, highly rhythmic manner. The technique is generally applied to dance tunes, perhaps originally as a means of remembering them when the church banned instruments.

Because for a time, at least, Scots traditional singers, particularly women, were more in evidence than their English counterparts, they have in turn had considerable influence over English revival singers. June Tabor and Frankie Armstrong, in particular, have cited members of the Stewart family as major early sources of inspiration.

Increasingly, singing traditions in Scotland may be falling victim to urbanization and industrialization, but renewed awareness of the richness of the tradition, combined with its growing popularity, virtually ensures its perpetuation in one form or another.

S·E·L·E·C·T·E·D R·E·C·O·R·D·I·N·G

The Muckle Sangs
(TANGENT 119/D)

A collection of recordings from the archives of the School of Scottish Studies, with an emphasis on Scots variants of the Child ballads, sung by leading Scottish source singers.

Jeannie Robertson

Jeannie Robertson was so imposing a figure in the field of traditional Scottish music that she virtually dwarfs all others.

Born in 1908 into a family of travelers, she experienced some of the travelers' life in her early years, including their rich heritage of traditional music and song, before settling in Aberdeen. Music was part of her daily experience and an integral part of her life. Married to Donald Higgins, a well-known piper and fiddler, she was also a member of the celebrated Stewart family of musicians, and already well known in her own district for her formidable singing talent when Hamish Henderson encountered her in 1953. Her discovery consummated Henderson's search for a major traditional source of folk song in rural northwestern Scotland, for Robertson, who had acquired most of her considerable repertoire from her mother and grandmother, was living evidence of the continuity of the folk song tradition.

Robertson was renowned as a storyteller as well as a singer, and in 1968 she was awarded an MBE for her contributions to the field of traditional music. She was truly an inspiration to countless members of the revival, and it is tragic that she never received more than a fraction of the recognition she deserved. Although venerating her as a source of material, many of her admirers lifted her songs wholesale, never even citing her as their source and never sharing with her any of the profits from their pursuits.

Though the last years of her life were marred by the effects of a stroke, her influence remains alive, not only through her daughter, Lizzie Higgins, a fine singer in her own right, but through the legend she left behind. Her singing belonged to a grand tradition, and she employed her rich, exquisitely controlled contralto in a most dramatic manner, infusing the old ballads with the very spirit and life that has kept them alive throughout the centuries.

S·E·L·E·C·T·E·D   R·E·C·O·R·D·I·N·G

The Great Scots Traditional Ballad Singer
(TOPIC 12T96)

A selection of ballads, all unaccompanied, this is a representative sampling of her singing, and well balanced between the big ballads and lighter material. Not only highly enjoyable, it demonstrates beyond question why Jeannie Robertson is still accorded such elevated stature, even nearly a decade after her death.

The Stewarts of Blairgowrie

There's scarcely a singer of traditional music in Scotland who hasn't at one time mentioned one of the Stewart family as a source of songs. For the Stewarts, a large clan of travelers, not only can boast a disproportionate number of fine singers and musicians among their ranks but a vast repertoire as well.

Although the great Jeannie Robertson was a Stewart on her mother's side, the best known of the Stewarts themselves probably is Belle, who was born in 1906 beside the River Tay. Belle was "discovered" as the result of one of her original songs, which had entered the tradition and caught the attention of Hamish Henderson in 1954. Henderson's fellow researcher from the School of Scottish Studies followed leads to Blairgowrie, where he encountered Belle, her husband Alex, and daughters Sheila and Cathie.

Belle Stewart's singing tends to be somewhat lighthearted, although simultaneously well controlled and straightforward. Her voice is marked by clarity of tone, and she makes subtle use of ornamentation, incorporating it masterfully into the song and melody. Through the revival, Belle, Alex, Sheila, and Cathie became well known to club and festival audiences.

S·E·L·E·C·T·E·D   R·E·C·O·R·D·I·N·G·S

The Travelling Stewarts
(TOPIC 12TS179)
•
Belle Stewart:
Queen Among the Heather
(TOPIC 12TS307)

The Travelling Stewarts, which includes Jeannie Robertson and Lizzie Higgins in addition to other members of the Stewart clan, demonstrates just how extensive a contribution the Stewarts have made to traditional music. High points include the late Alex Stewart's piping, as well as excellent performances by individual members of the family's various branches, notably a series of pipe tunes played on whistle and mouth organ. Belle Stewart's solo album documents the range of both her singing and repertoire. It is obvious that she enjoys singing, a quality that in turn transfers itself to the listener and makes this record of unaccompanied singing a delight.

Jimmy McBeath

Although he died in the early 1970s, Jimmy McBeath is still remembered as one of Scotland's finest traditional singers. Born in 1894, McBeath was among the last people to work under the exploitative bothy system, and, not surprisingly, much of his extensive repertoire was made up of bothy ballads. McBeath forsook the hard life of the farm servant to enlist in the army, and served in World War I and in Ireland. After his discharge, he earned his living through a series of menial jobs and, in time, through street singing.

In 1951 Hamish Henderson, collecting with Alan Lomax, discovered him and recorded his singing. McBeath rapidly became an important figure in the Scots revival, appearing at concerts and festivals, and regaling audiences with his lively performances.

McBeath was an energetic, gruff-voiced singer who favored humorous songs as well as the bothy ballads he was famous for. Whichever he sang, though, he delivered them with great pleasure, and was as well loved for his engaging personality as for his singing.

S·E·L·E·C·T·E·D R·E·C·O·R·D·I·N·G

Bound to Be a Row
(TOPIC 12TS303)

Recorded late in McBeath's life, this album has a more intimate tone than his performances would have, but it includes an excellent assortment of songs, and he gives a splendid performance.

Revival Singers

The line between source and revival singers may not be as clearly defined in Scotland as it is in England, primarily because of Scotland's history of patronage for musicians, but the modern professional folk singer is essentially removed from the traditional sources. Scots revival musicians, like their English cousins, hail mainly from urban environments. Archie Fisher, for example, didn't encounter folk song until he was in his teens, but went on to become one of the most popular and influential figures on the folk scene. Dick Gaughan and Jean Redpath, in contrast, were exposed to traditional music when they were growing up, although other types of music were just as much in evidence.

Like the best revival musicians anywhere, those in Scotland have transformed the musical traditions into something more through their skills as musicians. Archie Fisher has distinguished himself as a songwriter as well as a singer, and Dick Gaughan is as well known for his guitar style as he is for his distinctive singing.

Scottish revival singers not only have demonstrated taste, integrity, and artistry in their music but have been a driving force behind the dissemination, acceptance, and popularity of the Anglo-Celtic tradition.

Dick Gaughan

One of the most evocative singers in Scotland and indeed the British Isles, Dick Gaughan is an immense talent, one of the most respected musicians on the scene, if not always the most accessible.

Gaughan hails from Leith, of Irish and Scots stock. Because his family had no radio or television when he was growing up, musical gatherings provided entertainment instead. His grandparents and parents were all musicians, and his father was involved in the skiffle movement. It was as a result of his father's interest in skiffle that Gaughan himself developed an interest in folk song. He began to study it from an academic point of view; it didn't occur to him to sing the songs he was studying until around 1965, when he heard one of Ewan MacColl's radio programs. Gaughan became aware that the music was being performed, and he began to frequent the pubs where people were singing. The experience was overwhelming, and gradually he started singing himself.

In 1970 Gaughan went to London, and in 1972 his first solo album was released, to much acclaim. Although his reputation as a solo performer was growing, he joined his friend Aly Bain as a member of Boys of the Lough. Gaughan's strong singing aided the group's vocal work, and his guitar playing contributed to their instrumental side, but he returned to solo work when the strains of travel grew too great.

Still attracted to group work, however, in 1976 Gaughan became a member of the electric group Five Hand Reel, which was the Scottish counterpart of groups like Steeleye Span, although with closer ties to traditional music. Gaughan's stint with the band ended when his daughter was injured in an auto accident, and in time the group disbanded, but Gaughan's participation frequently is cited as the band's primary strength. While a member of Five Hand Reel, Gaughan still found time to record three solo albums. More recently, Gaughan has been the prime mover behind the Perform organization, whose aim is to increase communication between people involved in any way with the performance of folk music.

Dick Gaughan is a powerful and moving singer, but he has little of the softness that characterizes the singing of artists like Archie Fisher, or Andy Stewart of Silly Wizard. His style tends instead toward a rougher sound, and the lyrics frequently are difficult to understand because much of the time he sings in the Scottish Lowlands dialect. He is capable of great gentleness and great strength, at once subtle and bold, and few singers anywhere can match the nuances of his singing while offering such powerful delivery. Gaughan himself has said that his style is closer to the Irish than the Scots, an observation borne out by his heavier use of vocal ornamentation.

Gaughan's guitar playing is as distinctive as his singing. Through the use of a flat pick, he has created a highly syncopated, melodic style that can easily equal the intricacies of the foremost finger-style guitarists on the scene.

Dick Gaughan's talent easily places him with the best the folk scene in Britain has to offer. His music may not always be as easy to listen to as other singers', but it is well worth the (slightly) extra effort that may be required to appreciate it.

S·E·L·E·C·T·E·D R·E·C·O·R·D·I·N·G·S

Kist o' Gold
(TRAILER 2103)
•
Handful of Earth
(TOPIC 12TS419; ADVENT 3602)
•
Coppers and Brass
(TOPIC 12TS315)

Until *Handful of Earth* was released, *Kist o' Gold* was considered by many to be the definitive Dick Gaughan album. And it is a pleasing album that shows Gaughan at his best. But *Handful of Earth* is in a class by itself. Accompanied by Brian McNeill on fiddle and Phil Cunningham on keyboards, Gaughan has produced a remarkable record, from the bitter power of "Erin Go Bragh" to the wistful "The Snows They Melt the Soonest," and reveals his full range as a musician. *Handful of Earth* is to Gaughan's career what *Penguin Eggs* is to Nic Jones's, and likewise an essential part of any collection of British music. *Coppers and Brass* is a stunning selection of Scots and Irish dance music, which Gaughan plays on guitar.

Archie Fisher

To call Archie Fisher a singer would be like calling Woody Allen a comedian. True, he is a singer of tremendous warmth, just as Allen is a gifted humorist, but the convenient label allows little room for mention of either man's multifaceted talent. Not only is Fisher a masterful instrumentalist as well as a singer, but perhaps more significant, he is a writer of insightful and finely crafted songs.

Fisher's background is urban; he was born and raised in Glasgow, where he first encountered traditional music, when he was in his teens. Along with his sisters Cilla and Ray, he became known for his interpretation of traditional material.

Although Fisher's singing tends to be gentle, he nonetheless turns out a strong and compelling performance. He lacks the flamboyance of, say, Vin Garbutt, and is smoother than Dick Gaughan, but by no means can be considered colorless.

His style is lyrical and has been influenced by the best of the source singers and interpreters.

Fisher's guitar playing likewise isn't as dramatic as that of some of his peers, but it's always appropriate to the material, frequently inventive, and marked by just enough intricacy to be lively and interesting without upstaging his singing or material.

Fisher's repertoire is immersed in tradition, and nowhere is this more evident than in his songwriting. In virtually every case, his songs evoke traditional forms, even when reflecting contemporary concerns. His subjects range from the magical to the encroachment of industrialization on rural life. Invariably, his lyrics are intelligent and perceptive, and he has an unerring sense of melody that infuses his compositions with a beauty not often found in contemporary songs.

Archie Fisher is an influential and popular performer and something of a yardstick for measuring the tasteful interpretation of folk song not only in Scotland but throughout Britain and the United States as well.

S·E·L·E·C·T·E·D R·E·C·O·R·D·I·N·G·S

Will Ye Gang, Love
(TOPIC 12TS277)
•
The Man with a Rhyme
(FOLK-LEGACY FSS-61)

You can't go wrong with either one of these records. The Topic album contains somewhat lusher arrangements—which both enhance and hinder the material, as Fisher's voice is complemented by the rich sounds but occasionally is overwhelmed by them. *The Man with a Rhyme* benefits from simpler arrangements and a healthier dose of Fisher's own excellent songs.

Cilla Fisher and Artie Trezise

Cilla Fisher is the youngest of the Fisher family and, like her brother Archie and her sister Ray, one of the finest singers in Scotland. She performs with her husband, Artie Trezise, and they are one of the most popular duos of the revival.

The music of Cilla Fisher and Artie Trezise is characterized by great energy and superb technique. Cilla's singing in particular stands out, with Trezise's guitar accompaniment and singing usually forming more of a backdrop. His subdued guitar work is never intrusive, and his singing is pleasant if on the sweet side, but Cilla's voice and her interpretation of the songs is virtually flawless, marked by freshness and vigor and at the same time richness and purity of tone.

Although Fisher and Trezise concentrate on traditional material, they are not loath to include music by contemporary songwriters; they have recorded Stan Rogers's "Jeannie C," for example. (Ironically, Rogers's version of Cilla's brother Archie's "Witch of the West-mer-land" is one of his most requested numbers.) And the kind of lively and inventive music Cilla Fisher and Artie Trezise produce remains appealing over many hearings.

S·E·L·E·C·T·E·D R·E·C·O·R·D·I·N·G·S

Cilla and Artie
(TOPIC 12TS405)
•
For Foul Day and Fair
(FOLK-LEGACY FSS-69)

An impressive cast of supporting musicians appears on *Cilla and Artie,* including Alistair Anderson, Johnny and Phil Cunningham, and Brian McNeill, and although their contribution is incalculable, it is still Cilla's singing that stands out above all. The Folk-Legacy release is delightful as well, but *Cilla and Artie* is one of those records you can't stop playing, not only because of its varied material and inventive arrangements, but because the level of musicianship all around is stunning.

Jean Redpath

Jean Redpath is, quite simply, without peer among singers of traditional song. Her mastery of her craft is so complete that perhaps more than any other singer, she has the power to evoke great emotion in her audience.

Redpath comes from a home in which music of all kinds was always in evidence, but she received her only formal musical training in school. Despite her exposure to the "great" classical music of the Western world, traditional music was always first in her affections. Hamish Henderson introduced her to the singing of Jeannie Robertson and material that has remained in her repertoire, and she became actively involved in the Folk Song Society in Edinburgh.

Redpath concentrates almost exclusively on traditional material, usually Scottish. She is highly informed about her music, but attributes her knowledge to an interest in the material rather than any desire to pursue the academic study of folk song. "Primarily I sing," she has said. "I like to sing. Everything else is sort of a side issue."

Yet it is her well-informed delivery that makes her live performances even more of a delight than her albums. She has a relaxed and outgoing manner onstage, with a bright sense of humor that is belied by the largely serious nature of the songs she sings.

Although Redpath resides full time in the US, she returns regularly to Scotland. "I'd get a little phoney if I spent ten years over here and never set foot back in Scotland and claimed to know something about the Scottish language or the Scottish singing tradition," she once said.

And Redpath is anything but phoney. Her approach to her material is straightforward but highly sensitive, a quality that is augmented by her superb vocal technique. She has a sweet but somewhat husky contralto, which she controls perfectly, hitting every note squarely and with rich, expressive vibrato. She makes sparing but effective use of ornamentation, singing unaccompanied or accompanying herself on guitar; on record she usually is joined by a cellist and various other musicians. Yet always it is her lovely singing that dominates.

One of the more interesting projects in which Redpath has been involved has been the compilation and recording of the songs of Robert Burns, the legendary Scots poet. Burns's poems frequently were lyrics to songs, and over the centuries they were separated from their melodies, much as the Child ballads were . Along with composer Serge Hovey, who has researched the songs and written the arrangements, Redpath has created a body of music unprecedented in Scottish music.

S·E·L·E·C·T·E·D R·E·C·O·R·D·I·N·G·S

Song of the Seals
(PHILO PH 1054)
•
Lowlands
(PHILO PH 1066)
•
The Songs of Robert Burns, Volume 1
(PHILO PH 1037)

Jean Redpath is remarkably consistent in the quality of her performances, and for that reason any of these albums is a safe bet, as, indeed, any of her efforts would be. *Song of the Seals* and *Lowlands* are collections of primarily traditional songs, underscored by understated accompaniments and Redpath's flawless singing. *The Songs of Robert Burns* is the first volume in what will eventually be a 15-record series. The music has less of a "folk" feeling to it, mainly because of accompaniments that incorporate chamber music, but this and the other volumes in the series are a remarkable blend of scholarship and creativity and pleasing to listen to if not quite as moving as Redpath's treatment of traditional material.

Groups

Although Scotland is rich in both instrumental and vocal traditions, combining the two in musical ensembles is a fairly recent phenomenon. Gaining impetus partly from the English revival and even more from such Irish bands as Planxty and the Bothy Band, younger Scottish musicians have begun banding together to produce music that speaks to both the tradition and to modern life.

The rise of modern Scottish folk bands began during the 1960s, with such groups as the Corries and the Ian Campbell Folk Group, heirs to skiffle, who drew their inspiration from the other bands popular at the time in Britain and the United States. It was the Clutha, however, a semiprofessional group formed in 1963, that gave a better indication of the direction Scottish bands were headed.

Since the mid-1970s a number of groups have formed that combine traditional and modern influences in fresh, innovative ways. These newer bands play not only traditional tunes and songs but original material that evokes the older traditions. They are able to adapt the traditions more freely because the use of amplified instruments affords them more options. The advent of electric instruments in a folk context has meant that the bagpipes, for example, long a solo instrument or played only with other bagpipes, can be combined with different instrumentation because amplification enables those other instruments to be heard over the din of the pipes.

Most of the Scottish bands are a far cry from the folk-rock groups that proliferated in England during the 1970s; yet their willingness to experiment, coupled with their respect for tradition, has lent them a uniquely modern air.

The Battlefield Band

It's hard to believe that when the Battlefield Band first formed in Glasgow in mid-1969, its repertoire consisted mainly of Leonard Cohen and Bob Dylan songs. Yet the group has had the same kind of fitful history that has marked similar groups, and along with its changes in lineup have come changes in orientation. At times numbering six, other times only three, the group has centered around fiddle player Brian McNeill and keyboard player Alan Reid. Although women have sometimes been included in the group, the current Battlefield Band consists only of McNeill, Reid, piper Duncan MacGillivray, and Northumbrian native Ged Foley.

The Battlefield Band's sound is governed largely by MacGillivray's distinguished piping along with McNeill's fiddle playing and Reid's use of synthesizer, electric piano, and pedal organ, three instruments that raised some eyebrows when they were added but have come to be accepted as an appropriate and valuable part of the group's lineup.

The band's music is lively and anchored in tradition, while at the same time displaying elements of more recent musical developments. As Foley once explained their music, "It's tried and tested, really. And yet what you can actually do with it is limitless." Reid manages to use his electric keyboards in an altogether artful way, only enhancing the impeccable music of his cohorts. Duncan MacGillivray's piping is first-rate, and Alan Reid's singing stands out in any performance. Brian McNeill, known primarily as a fiddler, and a fine one at that, is also adept at concertina and virtually any fretted instrument. Ged Foley excels at mandolin but is conversant with the Northumbrian smallpipes as well. Altogether, the group plays at least 17 instruments on stage.

Because all members of the group are accomplished musicians, the Battlefield Band ranks among the best of its kind and has achieved the near impossible—crossover appeal to pop fans. The group opened for Mike Oldfield during a tour of Europe, to the resounding approval of Oldfield's fans. The band continues to concentrate on Scottish traditional music, with a few original compositions thrown in besides. Although not as relentlessly driving as the Tannahill Weavers, the Battlefield Band is nonetheless an exciting and powerful group of talented and tasteful musicians, and their music, as Brian McNeill once put it, is "just good music. It's the essence of live music. It's got rhythm. It's got guts."

S·E·L·E·C·T·E·D R·E·C·O·R·D·I·N·G·S

Home Is Where the Van Is
(TEMPLE TP005; FLYING FISH FF-250)
•
The Story So Far
(TEMPLE TP007)

Home Is Where the Van Is, a solid album reflecting the Battlefield Band's current lineup, reveals the present configuration to be stronger instrumentally than vocally—which hasn't always been the case. *The Story So Far* is, as you might expect, a "best of " album, tracing the evolution of the group through numerous personnel changes. It is not as cohesive as *Home Is Where the Van Is* but is particularly valuable as a guide to other Battlefield Band albums. Just choose what you like and then buy the record produced by that particular incarnation of the group.

The Tannahill Weavers

Subtlety may not be their long suit, but there's no denying the sheer energy and drive of the Tannahill Weavers, a quartet dominated by the piping of Alan MacLeod. Like many groups, their lineup has changed numerous times; they have been in existence since the late 1970s and at various times have been a quintet as well.

Although the Tannahill Weavers have been the object of some mild abuse in the press for their hard-driving approach, their music is enormously compelling. They are an extremely tight band, vocally as well as instrumentally, and while their close harmonies at times are breathtaking, it is their forceful instrumentals that are most apt to capture your attention. Like the Battlefield Band, their sound is shaped by the Highland bagpipes, but their sound is more commercial and lacking Battlefield's strong solo singing.

Although the music of the Tannahill Weavers is rooted firmly in tradition, it nonetheless has a contemporary feel, part of a continuing tradition rather than the strict preservation of the old. It isn't suited to casual listening, however, because it's sure to insinuate itself into your consciousness and take over whatever you're doing.

S·E·L·E·C·T·E·D R·E·C·O·R·D·I·N·G·S

The Tannahill Weavers
(PLANT LIFE PLR 017; GREEN LINNET SIF 3101)
•
Tannahill Weavers IV
(PLANT LIFE PLR 028; GREEN LINNET SIF 3102)

Despite some quieter moments, these are not the kind of albums you would play when you're in the mood for something soft and romantic, but they're great fun. There's some variation in personnel, but each record features a fairly similar mix of rousing jigs, reels, strathspeys and marches, along with impeccably harmonized, ballads and songs. *The Tannahill Weavers* reflects the group as a quintet, but the loss of numbers has little or no bearing on the music, as evidenced by *Tannahill Weavers IV.*

Silly Wizard

Nearly all the Scottish bands of note can boast excellent instrumentalists and at least one or two fine singers, but only Silly Wizard has all that and Andy Stewart. Stewart, one of the Stewart family of Blairgowrie, where he grew up, not only is the group's enormously entertaining onstage spokesman but one of the finest younger singers in Scotland and, increasingly, an accomplished songwriter as well.

Silly Wizard came together in 1972, although at the time only Gordon Jones, who plays guitar, and Johnny Cunningham, until recently the group's fiddle player, were part of the lineup. Stewart joined in 1974; and Martin Hadden, who plays bass, and Phil Cunningham, the band's superb keyboard player, joined in 1976. Silly Wizard has suffered its series of personnel changes, like many other Scottish groups, but comparatively speaking, its past has been stabler than the others', and Stewart, Jones, Hadden, and Phil Cunningham continue to form the core of the band. Silly Wizard includes no pipes but is distinguished by extensive use of accordion, and Stewart, although primarily a singer, also doubles as the group's banjo and whistle player.

Silly Wizard's music reflects a combination of influences, and the band itself is very representative of the younger generation of Scottish musicians; raised on the Beatles and rock and roll, they have chosen to concentrate on traditional material while incorporating modern elements into their music. They are not afraid of experimentation, including the use of electric instruments, but always they remain responsive to the requirements of the music, acutely aware that the synthesizer, for example, or the electric bass must be played in a manner consistent with the material.

Approximately half the band's repertoire is original, but because it is so firmly entrenched in tradition, it could easily be mistaken for traditional music. Stewart has, in fact, adapted and rewritten a number of traditional songs. The band strives for a balance between songs and tunes, and their music explores a wider range than either the Tannahill Weavers' or the Battlefield Band's. They are as capable of rousing instrumentals as either group, but the fundamental integrity of their slower numbers surpasses other groups and reflects, above all, their supreme sensitivity to traditional music.

S·E·L·E·C·T·E·D R·E·C·O·R·D·I·N·G·S

Caledonia's Hardy Sons
(HIGHWAY SHY 7004)
•
So Many Partings
(HIGHWAY SHY 7010)
•
Wild and Beautiful
(HIGHWAY SHY 7016)
•
Andy Stewart:
By the Hush
(HIGHWAY SHY 7018)

It's simply a matter of taste which of these LPs appeals most to you. *Caledonia's Hardy Sons* and *So Many*

Partings are the group's first two recorded efforts for Highway and sheer pleasure throughout. The first emphasizes vocal music more than the second, but there is enough of each on either album to strike a comfortable balance. *Wild and Beautiful* is marked by further use of amplified instruments, particularly on the second side, which is a medley of songs and tunes that builds to an intense and powerful crescendo. Stewart's solo album is an excellent work, featuring his usual blend of traditional and original material. His is a sweet singing style, but, happily, it is seldom cloying and often intensely moving. Stewart is not a singer of Dick Gaughan's magnitude, but in any other comparison, he comes off very well.

Ossian

It's no surprise that Ossian boasts an enormous following both in Europe and in Scotland. Although their music is far more restrained than that of either Silly Wizard, the Battlefield Band, or the Tannahill Weavers, their rare mix of instruments, including harp and uilleann pipes, and their careful arrangements make them most listenable.

Formed by ex-members of the folk-rock group Contraband, Ossian originally consisted of four musicians playing Celtic harp, uilleann pipes, whistle, fiddle, cello, guitar, cittern, mandolin, flute, and dulcimer, but by their fourth album, they had acquired a fifth member, rounding out their already satisfying sound. One of their major assets is their lead singer, Tony Cuffe, whose relaxed, unaffected singing is a perfect counterpoint to the group's precise instrumental work. It's too bad he isn't featured more on their albums.

The majority of Ossian's music is traditional, but their later recordings include some composed and original material as well, and their fourth album features the soundtrack they wrote for a short film about the island of Iona.

Although Ossian is based in Glasgow, the addition of harp and whistle lends their music a somewhat Irish character, similar in many ways to the sound of the Irish group Clannad. But whatever its label, it is exceptionally beautiful and, even if quieter than that of other Scottish groups, never lacking tension and energy.

S·E·L·E·C·T·E·D R·E·C·O·R·D·I·N·G·S

St. Kilda Wedding
(IONA 001)
•
Seal Song
(IONA 002)
•
Dove Across the Water
(IONA 004)

Although they all present a similar type of music, these albums trace the evolution of the group. On *Seal Song,* for example, they lost Billy Ross, but gained Tony Cuffe. All are excellent, but particularly noteworthy are "Tae the Beggin' " on *Dove Across the Water* and "Corn Rigs" on *Seal Song;* the vocal work, in general, is stronger on Ossian's later albums.

Songwriters

Although contemporary songwriters composing in the folk idiom sometimes are seen as the black sheep of the folk scene, in Scotland, art song and traditional song have long been interwoven, and the songwriter's role has virtually been defined by the culture itself.

From ancient times, through the 17th century, the Celtic bards were prominent figures in Scottish culture. Trained in their art for many years, the bards were part poet, part shaman, and served the chiefs of the clans by writing poetry and songs for important events.

Even later on, literature continued to be associated with traditional music. The renowned poet Robert Burns, active during the latter half of the 18th century, not only was a folk song collector but a songwriter as well. Many of his poems were written as lyrics for songs, and Burns also wrote words for some of composer and fiddler Niel Gow's tunes.

More recently, writers such as Hamish Henderson and the late Matt McGinn have left their mark, Henderson writing songs with a distinctly traditional flavor and McGinn known primarily for topical material.

The younger generation of songwriters currently active in Scotland call upon all these precedents while at the same time infusing their songs with contemporary sensibilities. Singer Archie Fisher, for example, one of the finest Scots songwriters, mainly emulates traditional forms, even when dealing with contemporary issues and subjects. Robin Williamson, on the other hand, can be viewed as a successor to the ancient bards, a role he has essentially created for himself by steeping himself in Celtic history and lore. Eric Bogle, however, now a citizen of Australia, focuses on social and interpersonal concerns, much as the topical songwriters of the sixties did, but Bogle approaches his subjects with far greater sensitivity.

Clearly Scotland's history of patronage for music has established a place for songwriters within the folk scene, and the result is modern music well integrated with musical traditions.

Robin Williamson

Although Robin Williamson is a native Scot, he has come to view himself and his music as belonging to the broader pan-Celtic world, incorporating elements of the Celtic culture from the many countries where the Celts eventually settled.

A skilled poet, singer, storyteller, songwriter, and multi-instrumentalist, Williamson still is probably best known as the cofounder of the Incredible String Band, a 1960s group that combined folk, rock, jazz, and Indian influences in a sound redolent of the sensibilities of that decade. Since the breakup of the Incredible String Band in the early 1970s, however,

Williamson has been steadily involved in a series of projects from coauthoring a suspense novel to the study of ancient Celtic history and incorporating it into his creative efforts, which have been considerable.

Williamson is now a resident of California, and most recently was involved in another group—Robin Williamson and his Merry Band, which disbanded in 1979. The group, which included champion harper Sylvia Woods, played mainly Williamson's neo-Celtic compositions, with a few music hall and novelty pieces sprinkled in. Since the Merry Band's breakup, Williamson has performed solo, a situation that enables him to showcase his many talents. Although he is highly conversant with a variety of instruments, including harp, cittern, whistle, button accordion, fiddle, guitar, and border pipes, his main influence is as a songwriter and Celtic figurehead. Yet with the possible exception of "First Girl I Loved," made popular (after a change of gender) by Judy Collins, his songs are far from mainstream pop, yet neither are they folk-style pastiches either. Marked by a distinctly contemporary flavor, they are often a series of images, dreamlike and fantastic, and not necessarily cohesive or even coherent. Frequently they are simply mood pieces.

S·E·L·E·C·T·E·D R·E·C·O·R·D·I·N·G

Songs of Love and Parting
(FLYING FISH FF 257)

Although a solo effort, this album is one of Williamson's most accessible. With lush arrangements and more conventional songs, Williamson seems to be hitting his stride as a writer and arranger. It may take a little time to grow on you, but patience will be rewarded for it is, in the end, a very pretty record.

Eric Bogle

No one with even the most tenuous connections with the folk scene in Britain or the United States can have failed to be touched by the songs of Eric Bogle. From the magnificent "No Man's Land" and the shattering "And the Band Played Waltzing Matilda" to the wistful "Leaving Nancy," his music has found its way into the performances and onto the albums of many of the leading folk musicians on both sides of the Atlantic, not to mention Bogle's adopted homeland, Australia.

Bogle is a songwriter acutely aware of his fellow human beings and is quick to come to the defense of the underdogs—the poor, the old, the oppressed, and persecuted—and has a genius for personalizing his material in a way that begs response from the listener. Many of his songs reflect his socialist leanings, but never in a didactic way and always indirectly. Although his topical songs tend to be his strongest, his oeuvre includes a significant number of songs confronting the issues of interpersonal relations as well. He writes about subjects that move him emotionally, whether they're things he's experienced himself or merely things he's heard about.

Bogle has said that the words always come first in his songwriting, a fact that in retrospect seems evident, as his lyrics consistently are intelligent and conform to an extremely high standard. Yet his songs are melodic as well, proof of his mastery of his craft.

As a performer, a role he doesn't necessarily covet, Bogle is low-key, never slick, but comfortable and engaging. He quickly captures the attention and loyalty of his audience, and he has said that while he admires people who have mastered their instruments, it means nothing if their performance has no heart, a dictum he obviously follows himself.

A former accountant, Bogle divided his time between Scotland and Australia for a while but eventually opted for permanent full-time residence in Australia, which, he found, was an environment more conducive to his writing.

Although his original material is the most interesting part of his repertoire, he also presents a few traditional songs, and songs by other contemporary songwriters as well. Yet he scrupulously avoids hackneyed material, a policy that keeps his albums and concert appearances fresh and intriguing.

S·E·L·E·C·T·E·D R·E·C·O·R·D·I·N·G·S

Now I'm Easy
(LARRIKIN LRF041)
•
With John Monroe:
Plain and Simple
(PLANT LIFE PLR 033)

Together, these two records pretty much cover Eric Bogle's best-known songs. *Now I'm Easy* features Bogle solo with the subtle backup of a studio band. The title tune is a tender account of a farmer's life, derived from a barroom conversation Bogle had with just such a man. There are many highlights, including his two "hits," "No Man's Land" and "And the Band Played Waltzing Matilda." *Plain and Simple* offers similar fare, although with the addition of several songs not composed by Bogle. You can't afford to overlook the work of this important songwriter.

IRELAND

The musical traditions of Scotland and Ireland have a great deal in common. Like Scotland's, Ireland's national music had its roots in the bardic tradition—the poets and musicians who served the nobility in ancient times. With the growth of Anglo influences, however, the bardic strain began to wane, and in the middle of the 17th century, the bardic schools were destroyed. As in Scotland, much of Ireland's music is authored, and the travelers have played a major role in its perpetuation and dissemination.

In general, however, Irish music has retained stronger ties with its Celtic origins; the Celtic influence is strongest in the Gaeltacht regions—those areas of the country where Irish is the first language. But that is not to say that English influence is lacking. On the contrary, the English influence on Irish music has been significant, as it has been in all areas of Irish life, and remains clearly discernible, especially in the area of song.

Irish music consists primarily of songs and dance tunes; little falls into other categories, although there are some instrumental pieces that were written purely for listening. Even airs, however, were usually composed to accommodate lyrics. Whether vocal or instrumental, though, the Irish musical tradition is solo and unaccompanied, focusing on the melody, which most often is modal. The instrumental music often has a circular construction, which means that the last phrase of the tune develops in such a way that the piece can be repeated indefinitely, or that the final note can lead into another tune—a characteristic that is important because Irish musicians tend to play two or three tunes back to back.

Although the Irish harp is the instrument most often associated with Irish traditional music in the public mind, in fact the traditional Irish harp is extinct, and the version that is widely played today, strung with gut, is not traditional, nor is the manner of playing it, since no one knows exactly how the ancient harps were played. The fiddle, uilleann pipes, whistle, and flute all are traditional, although how far back they date and in what form remains unknown. There are, however, ancient references to the pipes, fiddle, and whistle dating from around 1160.

It has been speculated that most of the tunes and airs preserved in the Irish tradition date to the last three centuries, particularly the latter 18th and early 19th centuries. Much of the instrumental music has been written down, and the earliest instance of this appears to date back to the 16th century. It wasn't until 1726, however, that an entire collection of Irish music was published, and the first collection of music taken down from traditional musicians didn't appear until late in the century.

In 1851, the first organization devoted to traditional music was founded. Called the Society for the Preservation and Publication of the Melodies of Ireland, it was the brainchild of George Petrie. The group foresaw the collection and classification of the countless unpublished airs in manuscript form and hoped to open a center in Dublin for collecting airs that people might send in to them. This was never realized, but Petrie's *Ancient Music of Ireland* was published in 1855, a collection of 147 airs and extensive notes. Further collections of Petrie's manuscripts were published after his death.

Other collectors of the 19th century included Patrick Weston Joyce; William Forde, first of his peers to use a systematic approach in handling his material, setting down variants of tunes; Dr. Henry Hudson, musical editor of two magazines; and James Goodman who probably was the best equipped of the lot to handle the subject, since he not only was able to read music, but was a native Irish speaker and a piper as well.

By far the greatest collector, however, was Francis O'Neill, the retired superintendent of police in Chicago around the turn of the century. A native of West Cork, O'Neill was an accomplished flute player and well qualified to handle the task of assembling traditional tunes. He was assisted by a police sergeant on the force named, coincidentally, James O'Neill, who actually transcribed the tunes. In 1903 the fruit of their labors was published, under the title *The Music of Ireland,* and contained 1,859 pieces. In 1907 O'Neill published a second book, this time exclusively dance tunes, taken mostly from his first book. Three additional books followed, making O'Neill certainly the most prolific of the collectors of Irish music, and establishing his position at the forefront of the field.

Because the Irish tradition is still vital, there has never been a place for a folk music revival per se in Ireland. But as in Scotland, the English and American revivals strengthened the existing tradition in Ireland and served to attract many of the younger people back to their native music. During the 1960s, a number of influential younger musicians emerged, and today, with informal musical sessions the order of the day, Irish traditional music is healthier than ever.

S·E·L·E·C·T·E·D R·E·C·O·R·D·I·N·G

The Lark in the Morning
(TRADITION TLP 1004)

A fine collection of traditional music played and sung by traditional musicians. Both English- and Irish-language traditions are represented, and the emphasis is on unaccompanied singing, although there are a few tunes included as well.

The Uilleann Pipes

The uilleann, or union, pipes are the most common type of pipe played in Irish music and contribute significantly to the overall sound of Irish instrumental music. The pipes in some form were probably known in 11th-century Ireland, and during the Tudor reign, pipes were in use in a military context, as well as for funerals. Through the 17th century, the pipes referred to in literature were undoubtedly the warpipes (Highland bagpipes), as the distinctly Irish form of pipes probably did not emerge until early in the 18th century, a point that is the object of some dispute.

The bag of the uilleann pipes, like that of the Northumbrian smallpipes, is inflated by means of a bellows, and consequently the instrument has a sweeter tone than the Highland bagpipes; the reeds are softer because they don't need to withstand the moisture introduced in the mouth-blown Scottish pipes, and the tone, in turn, is softer as well. The instrument is comprised of essentially 3 components in addition to the bag and bellows: the chanter, the pipe on which the melody is played; the drones, which are just what their name implies, and are pitched at bass, baritone, and tenor; and the regulators, which also number 3 and are used for playing simple chords and harmony.

While the uilleann pipes may be something of an acquired taste, they are an instrument of remarkable versatility. They are ideally suited to playing highly ornamented melodies; in fact, in piping, ornamentation is almost everything. To take advantage of this, the piper employs a number of techniques that are often emulated by musicians playing other instruments. Among the most common of these are the roll, a group of 3 grace notes, and the cran, a stuttering sound achieved through the use of grace notes to ornament the bottom and second notes on the chanter.

Fingering technique also affects the piping style. In open, or loose, fingering only those fingers necessary to sound the note are left on the chanter; in close, or tight, fingering only those fingers needed to sound the note are taken off the chanter. The effect is more legato with loose fingering; close fingering has the opposite effect, and close fingering is considered a more difficult way of playing.

Players of other instruments frequently cite pipers as having influenced their styles. Among those who have had the greatest impact on others, both pipers and nonpipers, have been the late Johnny Doran, a traveler and piper of considerable renown; Willie Clancy; and especially Leo Rowsome. Among the younger pipers, Liam O'Flynn of Planaty, and Paddy Keenan, formerly of the Bothy Band, are particularly worthy of note.

Like virtually all instruments used in Irish traditional music, the pipes are basically a solo instrument, so much the more so since the pipers can provide their own accompaniment through the regulators. More recently, however, pipes have been incorporated into bands and used quite effectively in ensemble playing.

Leo Rowsome

When it comes to piping, Leo Rowsome remains the standard for virtuosity. He was the leading exponent of piping in Ireland, and his influence was incalculable, bringing to the playing of the pipes a finesse and complexity seldom approached and never equalled.

Rowsome was born in 1903, the son and nephew of pipers. He began to study the instrument at an early age, under the instruction of his father and his uncle, and by the age of 13, he was learning the craft of pipe-making in his father's shop. At the age of 16, he became a teacher of piping at the School of Music, a position he held until his death in 1970. In 1925, when his father died, he took over the family pipe-making business and, despite the odds against him, turned the business into a profitable venture.

Rowsome not only was superlative as a solo piper, he played in bands with other instruments and was involved with several pipe bands. In 1936 he was a key figure in the reformation of the Pipers' Club, which had dissolved in 1924 as a result of the Irish civil war, and in 1958, when the international piping organization Na Piobairi Uilleann was formed, he was named joint chairman, along with Seamus Ennis.

Rowsome's style was highly distinctive, marked by fairly extensive use of the regulators, yet he never overused them, and the harmony they provided always punctuated the melody effectively. His playing was intricate, made even more so by the counterpoint between the legato chanter and the staccato regulators. Rowsome's style was less ornamented than some; he employed ornamentation to further the melody rather than to obscure it. Cranning was, however, one of his favorite devices, even though his style tended to be more legato than that of other players.

Clearly Leo Rowsome approached piping as a joyful activity, an idea that was borne out by his total absorption in the pipes. While other pipers might have seen the pipes as a hobby, he earned his living from them—through teaching, playing, and making them.

S·E·L·E·C·T·E·D R·E·C·O·R·D·I·N·G

Classics of Irish Piping, Volume 1
(TOPIC 12TS259)

If you're not sure whether you like the pipes, this may be the album to change your mind, for Rowsome's use of the regulators not only makes the music a trifle more accessible to ears accustomed to European music, but the sheer vitality of his playing bursts through. Although the cuts date back as far as the 1920s, the fidelity is remarkably clear. An excellent album and an excellent introduction to the instrument.

Willie Clancy

Although Willie Clancy was best known as a piper, he not only was an accomplished flute and whistle player, but a fine singer as well. Clancy, who hailed from County Clare, became interested in music as a result of his father's flute playing and singing. The older man had learned all his tunes from a blind traveling piper, and his reminiscences about the man in turn generated an interest in the pipes in his son. When Willie met with Johnny Doran, another well-known traveling piper, he received his first instruction on the pipes and began to seek out pipers all over the country, absorbing elements of their styles and gaining expertise.

Clancy's piping was strong and forthright; he had mastered the technique of close fingering on the chanter, which produced a crisp sound and lent his playing much of its power. His flute and whistle playing were equally impressive—lively, fluid, and energetic, and he employed piping-type ornamentation in his whistle playing, which infused the instrument with a complexity heard only when it was played by masters.

His song repertoire included many English songs, and he sang them in a warm full voice, but he once expressed wistfulness about wanting to learn songs in Irish.

Clancy died in 1973, but his playing has continued to exert an enormous influence over other musicians.

S·E·L·E·C·T·E·D R·E·C·O·R·D·I·N·G

Willie Clancy, The Minstrel from Clare
(TOPIC 12TS175)

An impressive, memorable album that shows Clancy's full range as a musician. The tunes on whistle and pipes as well as the songs all reveal him to have been a master of many trades, and will surely appeal to anyone even remotely interested in Irish music.

Seamus Ennis

Collector, producer, linguist and piper—Seamus Ennis was one of the most respected and influential figures on the Irish folk scene and has left an indelible mark on the revival in Britain as well.

Born in 1919 in North County Dublin, Ennis was the son of musical parents; his father played flute and fiddle and founded a pipe band, and his mother was a fiddle player. Ennis became interested in music early in life—his attraction to the uilleann pipes stemmed back to the old country pipers he heard at Dublin festivals—but he didn't begin to study the pipes until he was 13.

In the late 1930s, Ennis went to work at Three Candles Press, the imprint that had produced several collections of Irish music under the aegis of publisher and collector Colm O'Lochlainn; in 1942 he became involved with the Irish Folklore Commission, and began his career as a collector. He traveled the countryside, gathered songs, tunes, and stories in English and Irish, and ventured into Scotland as well.

In 1947 Ennis went to work for Radio Eireann as a collector, performer, and producer, collaborating with Alan Lomax at one point, and in 1951 Ennis moved to London to work for the BBC. In addition to collecting in England and Scotland, Ennis appeared on the BBC show "As I Roved Out" as producer, performer, and collector.

Despite his many activities, Ennis's piping continued unabated during this period. He performed at traditional gatherings of every description, proving his abilities as a singer, storyteller, and folklorist as well. From the late 1950s on, Ennis was engaged in independent performing, broadcasting, and translating in Britain, Ireland, and the United States.

Seamus Ennis was known for having a complete command of the pipes, proficient on both the chanter and the regulators. His style combined the legato and staccato qualities of the two predominant fingering styles. But his musicianship notwithstanding, his major lasting influence is likely to remain his collecting. Through his efforts, a huge body of material has been preserved, and the music of Ireland has won a position of prominence and popularity. He died in 1982.

S·E·L·E·C·T·E·D R·E·C·O·R·D·I·N·G·S

Forty Years of Irish Piping
(GREEN LINNET SIF 1000)
•
The Wandering Minstrel
(TOPIC 12TS250)

Forty Years of Irish Piping is a double album that traces Ennis's career as a musician. Although the emphasis clearly is on piping, Ennis's singing, whistle playing, and storytelling also are represented. The album suffers from inconsistent fidelity, owing largely to the wide range of years and technology that the collection spans. Because the record represents so long a period in so significant a figure's career, it's also unfortunate that the album notes aren't more extensive. *The Wandering Minstrel,* an album exclusively devoted to pipe music, benefits from modern fidelity. The subtleties of Ennis's playing come through, and detailed liner notes explain the tunes, which include hornpipes, reels, jigs, and slow airs.

Paddy Keenan

Paddy Keenan is probably best known as the piper in the Bothy Band, but he is highly acclaimed for his solo work as well. A native of Dublin, he is widely acknowledged as one of the finest of the younger generation of pipers—and with good reason. For in addition to having achieved phenomenal technical proficiency on this most difficult of instruments, Keenan is a marvelously inventive and innovative player, having devised several new piping techniques that add dimension and complexity to the playing of the instrument.

Keenan's style is modeled after that of the great traveling piper, Johnny Doran, with a wild but controlled quality and spare but effective use of the regulators. He is a master of both open and close fingering techniques, but what makes his playing most outstanding is its excitement; at times it is breathtaking, with a vigor seldom equalled, certainly never surpassed.

Keenan is the third generation of pipers in a highly musical family from Dublin. He began playing the pipes at the age of 12, although he had played the whistle for several years before that. His father drove him extremely hard in his study of the instrument, but with the result that Paddy Keenan is assuredly one of the greatest pipers of the present and perhaps any time.

S·E·L·E·C·T·E·D R·E·C·O·R·D·I·N·G·S

Paddy Keenan
(GAEL-LINN CEP 045)
•
With Paddy Glackin:
Doublin'
(TARA 2007)

Keenan's solo album is an impressive achievement, with skilled and tasteful playing by his father and brother, as well as Paddy Glackin on fiddle. It remains a showcase for Keenan, however. *Doublin'* is an enormously invigorating collaboration between Keenan and Glackin that has enjoyed great success commercially as well as artistically.

The Fiddle

The fiddle is perhaps more widely played than any other instrument in Ireland. It was probably used for dances before the pipes emerged in their present form; the fiddle itself developed in the 16th century, and it had been widely adopted by the 18th century. A great deal of Irish dance music was composed by fiddle players, but also significant was the influence of Scots fiddle music.

Irish fiddling is some of the most accomplished and exciting in the world, with a plethora of stylistic differences among regions and between individuals within those areas. Through radio and records, the distinctions between the regional styles have become somewhat blurred, as the styles are disseminated and assimilated, but certain differences persist. In Donegal, for example, the emphasis is on bowing; the action of the bow on the strings is more audible in the Donegal style than in others, and the treatment of the melody is more direct and less ornamented. Donegal's is a loud, driving style, marked by fairly even tempo and rhythm.

The Sligo style is softer and more ornate; the Sligo fiddler makes generous use of ornamentation in a rather flamboyant, showy style. The treatment of the individual notes tends to be more legato. The Sligo style is very much in evidence as a result of the influence of the famed Sligo fiddler of the 1920s, Michael Coleman.

The Clare style is similar to the Sligo, but not as showy and more rhythmic; the bowing style makes for a more staccato sound than Sligo's. Its leading exponent today is probably Bobby Casey. In West Limerick and North Kerry, players tend to lean hard on the bow and emphasize a strong rhythm.

Although the fiddle tradition, like that of all traditional instruments in Ireland, is a solo one, many recordings, particularly early ones, incorporate piano accompaniment into the cuts, often muddling the sound and the stylistic differences of the players. More recently, with the development of groups that play in arranged parts, the fiddle has been used as an accompaniment instrument and as part of an ensemble.

S·E·L·E·C·T·E·D R·E·C·O·R·D·I·N·G

The Wheels of the World
(SHANACHIE 33001)

A sampling of the great recordings of Irish musicians made in the 1920s. Included are some of the great fiddlers of the day, including Michael Coleman, Paddy Killoran, and James Morrison, although players of other instruments also are represented to a lesser degree.

Michael Coleman

Probably the leading influence on Irish fiddling today, Michael Coleman was from Sligo, the region noted for its ornamented fiddle style. His father was also a fiddler, reputedly with a bowing technique similar to his son's, and the Coleman home was a center for musical activity in the area.

At the age of 20, Coleman departed for the United States, and it was there that his star began to rise. Equally respected and revered in Ireland and in the United States as a result of his records, Coleman's playing came to influence not only other fiddle players but pipers, flute players, and accordion players as well. Although his style was firmly grounded in tradition, he embellished the melodies more than Sligo players traditionally had, creating in the process a wholly unique approach. While he was a gifted technician, what distinguished his playing most was its inventiveness. His style was strong and driving and distinctly musical.

Michael Coleman was in a class by himself as far as influence and innovation went, and echoes of his style can still be heard today in the playing of many young fiddle players, as well as other instrumentalists.

S·E·L·E·C·T·E·D R·E·C·O·R·D·I·N·G

The Legacy of Michael Coleman
(SHANACHIE 3302)

Even through the surface noise, an inevitable part of any recording from the 1920s or 1930s, Coleman's virtuosity is readily apparent. Like all of Coleman's recordings, those included here were made in the US. It's interesting to note that although the cuts are set off by piano accompaniment, the pianist often cannot keep up with Coleman's rapidfire approach to the tunes. All are played at top speed, making them real showpieces for his skill.

Kevin Burke

Best known as the fiddle player for the now-defunct Bothy Band, Kevin Burke is a fiddler of precise technique, sweet tone, and consummate taste.

Burke, who was raised in London, studied classical music for a while but cites Michael Coleman, Paddy Killoran, Bobby Casey, and Martin Byrnes as among his major influences. He first recorded in the US, with Arlo Guthrie, and played with Hoyt Axton, which no doubt reflects a broadminded approach to music.

Burke joined the Bothy Band in time for their second album, which was released in 1976, and remained with the group until its demise in 1979. While he was a member, he found time to record a solo album, and since the breakup, he has recorded with fellow ex-member Mícheál Ó Domhnaill and with former De Danann accordion player Jackie Daly.

Burke's playing is wonderfully expressive, characterized by a light touch, but sacrificing none of the spirit so strongly associated with Irish fiddle music. The Sligo influence shows in his uses of ornamentation, although it is nowhere nearly as extensive as that of Michael Coleman, for example. His music is exuberant but at the same time reflecting an undercurrent of restraint, a quality that has created a highly individual style.

S·E·L·E·C·T·E·D R·E·C·O·R·D·I·N·G·S

If the Cap Fits
(MULLIGAN LUN 021; GREEN LINNET SIF 3009)

•

With Mícheál Ó Domhnaill:
Promenade
(MULLIGAN LUN 028; GREEN LINNET SIF 3010)

•

With Jackie Daly:
Eavesdropper
(MULLIGAN LUN 039; GREEN LINNET SIF 3002)

If the Cap Fits is a thoroughly engaging collection of tunes; Burke is joined by Jackie Daly, Peter Browne, Paul Brady, Gerry O'Beirne, Donal Lunny, and Mícheál Ó Domhnaill. Inventive arrangements make it easy, warm, and appealing listening. The collaboration with Ó Domhnaill reflects the work both have been doing since the breakup of the Bothy Band. Although largely instrumental, it includes some of Ó Domhnaill's gentle singing, and won the Montreal Jazz Festival Grand Prix du Disque in 1980. *Eavesdropper* focuses on the solo and combined talents of Burke and Daly, although they are joined by Paul Brady and other assorted musicians. Their version of "The Blackbird" is worth the entire price of the album.

Tommy Peoples

Whereas Kevin Burke's playing tends to be somewhat lyrical, Tommy Peoples's, is aggressive. The original fiddle player with the Bothy Band, Peoples left after the group's first album.

Peoples, who is from Donegal, learned to play fiddle from his cousin Joe Cassidy and captures the Donegal style in his own, even while incorporating in it influences from a variety of areas. His fiddling is spare of ornamentation and strong on bowing; he uses the typical Donegal technique of short bow strokes, giving it a staccato feeling. Probably his most distinctive trait is his use of "stuttering" single-note triplets, much like the piping technique of cranning, which injects a jagged edge into his playing. His style is driving and direct; the melody stands out starkly. And because of its penetrating quality, Peoples's fiddle playing is unusually compelling.

S·E·L·E·C·T·E·D R·E·C·O·R·D·I·N·G

With Paul Brady:
The High Part of the Road
(SHANACHIE 29003)

Two great talents combine forces in this album of traditional tunes. Not only is Peoples's fiddle playing enormously invigorating, but Paul Brady provides wonderfully inventive and complementary accompaniments on the guitar. The result never fails to dazzle.

The Flute and Tin Whistle

The flute has been a popular instrument in Irish traditional music probably since the 18th century, possibly later. The traditional instrument is wooden, with a corresponding warm tone, and it remains the type in use today, as the possibilities for ornamenting the melody are greater than they are with the metal flute, which is unsuitable for rolling and sliding into notes, two common devices.

The tin whistle's place in Irish music on the other hand, is older, better established, and more firmly entrenched. The earliest whistles found date to the 13th century; made of bone, they were discovered in High Street in Dublin during a 1968 archaeological excavation. Ancient tales also tell of whistle players, although it isn't clear if the instrument involved bears any resemblance to today's tin whistle.

The whistle is one of the least expensive musical instruments, and that, coupled with its pleasing tone and ease of playing, is undoubtedly one reason for its prevalance. Although it is sometimes considered something of a toy, it is a bonafide musical instrument with great potential for versatility in the hands of a master. Most whistles today are made of metal with plastic mouthpieces that can be moved slightly to facilitate some degree of tuning.

Stylistically, the flute and whistle have a lot in common. The main influence on the way they are played has been piping, and there are two major ways in which they are approached. One style, favored in the western regions of Ireland, reflects a flowing, sustained delivery; embellishment of the melody takes precedence over rhythmic ornamentation, and the sound is fluid and legato. The other style is marked by tonguing, which in turn produces a staccato effect.

Matt Molloy

Born in County Roscommon, Matt Molloy learned to play the flute from his father. Truly a master of his instrument, he has produced some of the most stunning music to come out of Ireland.

As a result of his playing with Tommy Peoples, Molloy was already well known in Irish music circles when he joined the Bothy Band. But his participation in that group really brought him to the fore. His playing is significant for its remarkable clarity and intricacy. He has impressive breath control, enabling him to produce almost uninterrupted musical phrases, an ability that contributes immeasurably to his smooth style. His playing owes a clear debt to piping techniques, and he adapts the piping techniques in ways that are ever appropriate and seem as natural on the flute as on the pipes. Few can even approach his sensitivity and finesse.

After the Bothy Band dissolved, Molloy joined the re-formed Planxty for a while, then the Chieftains, with whom he has remained as a permanent member.

S·E·L·E·C·T·E·D R·E·C·O·R·D·I·N·G

Matt Molloy
(MULLIGAN LUN 004)

A remarkably beautiful album, not only for the airy delicacy of Molloy's flute but for Donal Lunny's excellent bouzouki accompaniment as well. There is a haunted quality to the music that is captured equally in the solo and accompanied numbers.

Mary Bergin

A native of Dublin, Mary Bergin was the product of a highly musical family and was encouraged at an early age to pursue a musical instrument. She selected the tin whistle, and through dedication and talent ended up winning the All-Ireland championship by the time she was in her late teens.

Bergin's whistle playing is, in a word, delightful—precise, delicate, and nimble. She has been influenced by Michael Coleman, Patsy Touhey (a piper), and Willie Clancy, and her outstanding breath control has made for a fluid, vigorous, style.

Bergin, who has performed with De Danann, now lives in the Connemara Gaeltacht, where she and her husband make instruments.

S·E·L·E·C·T·E·D R·E·C·O·R·D·I·N·G

Feadóga Stáin
(GAEL-LINN CEF 071; SHANACHIE 79006)

Sheer pleasure from start to finish, this record will make a convert out of anyone not sure they like Irish music. Accompanied by Alec Finn and Johnny "Ringo" McDonagh of De Danann, as well as playing solo, Bergin plays reels, jigs, hornpipes, and slow airs exquisitely and with great feeling. She is a complete master of that humblest of instruments.

The Accordion

The accordion has been somewhat controversial in certain traditional quarters. Like its free reed cousins the melodeon (from which it was derived) and the concertina (popular in County Clare), the accordion produces notes mechanically, by air that is passed through the metal reeds within, and some people feel that ornamentation not only is more difficult but less suitable than it is on such instruments as the whistle, fiddle, and pipes.

The melodeon grew to prominence toward the end of the last century, as the pipes were experiencing a decline. It was ideal for accompanying dances, particularly the set dances (quadrilles) that were growing in popularity at the time. The melodeon has a single row of ten buttons and two spoon-shaped keys for providing bass. Among its virtues is the fact that it is easy to play.

Unlike its forebear, the accordion is fully chromatic, due to the addition of another row of buttons. The accordion began to gain favor among traditional musicians late in the 1920s, eventually eclipsing the melodeon, and has remained a popular instrument.

There are essentially two styles of play. The first relates to the melodeon. Because the melodeon player had to change direction with the bellows to change notes, he did so often, creating a rhythmic effect. The phrasing was simple, and single and double grace notes contributed ornamentation, along with variation in the melody. This approach has been transferred to the accordion.

The other style of playing developed when younger players unacquainted with the melodeon took up the accordion. They used the inner row of buttons as the main one and the other for ornamentation; they could cover the outer button with the same finger they used on the inner row and were able to add increased ornamentation, including triplets, without changing direction with the bellows. This style is more legato and slurred, and the use of the basses enables harmonic accompaniment, which is essentially at odds with the traditional, melodic orientation of Irish music.

Be that as it may, the accordion is a significant part of Irish traditional music today, although less in evidence than the pipes, fiddle, and whistle.

Joe Cooley

Joe Cooley was one of the best-loved and most accomplished accordion players in Ireland. Originally from South Galway, he spent 20 years in the United States beginning in the early 1950s, and was influential there as well as back home in Ireland. As a young man he spent many hours listening to Johnny Doran play the pipes, and from him learned many tunes. After emigrating to America, he had a ceilí band in Chicago.

Joe Cooley was a strong player, with a joyous, expansive way of playing. Technically, he was a master, but the appeal of his music lies more in its emotional quality than in his technical skill.

Cooley died in Dublin in 1973, but left behind a lasting impression on fine younger accordion players such as Martin O'Connor and Tony MacMahon.

S·E·L·E·C·T·E·D R·E·C·O·R·D·I·N·G

Cooley
(GAEL-LINN CEF 044)

Issued after his death, this is a collection of recordings made at various times in Cooley's career, the majority made late in his life. Although Cooley's playing is a delight, one of the most outstanding qualities of the album is the "session" atmosphere it manages to convey. Occasionally Cooley can be heard introducing tunes, and the listener has the feeling of being an observer at the sessions where the music was recorded.

Joe Burke

Joe Burke is considered by many to be the finest exponent of the Irish accordion today. A native of Galway, Burke came to the instrument at the age of four, through the encouragement of his uncle. Although Burke is essentially self-taught, he was highly influenced by his neighbors, the Downey family, and by Paddy O'Brien of Tipperary. In 1959 and 1960, Burke won the All-Ireland Senior accordion championship.

Joe Burke's playing is marked by a precise technique and, at the same time, a freewheeling blend of playfulness and strength, exuberance and restraint. His music is wonderfully buoyant and smooth, with an infectious quality that reveals the control of a true master.

In 1970 Burke was named RTE's Traditional Musician of the Year.

S·E·L·E·C·T·E·D R·E·C·O·R·D·I·N·G

With Andy McGann and Felix Dolan:
The Funny Reel
(SHANACHIE 29012)

An excellent collection of tunes played on accordion and fiddle (the latter courtesy of McGann) and set to Felix Dolan's tasteful piano accompaniment. Burke's technique is unsurpassed, and he, McGann, and Dolan produce highly enjoyable music together.

Martin O'Connor

Although Martin O'Connor's grandparents played the melodeon, and he learned a lot from them, he cites piper Patsy Touhey as a major influence on his accordion playing, a point that is borne out by his tasteful and controlled use of ornamentation.

A native of Galway, O'Connor plays the two-row button accordion masterfully, with a sensitive balance between ornamentation and clean, simple melody. Never obscuring the tune, O'Connor nonetheless captures the intricacy of pipe tunes and fiddle music. His approach is innovative and infused with freedom and vibrancy, while at the same time revealing flawless technique. O'Connor achieves a remarkable flowing quality on what so often is a basically staccato instrument.

S·E·L·E·C·T·E·D R·E·C·O·R·D·I·N·G

The Connachtman's Rambles
(MULLIGAN LUN 027; GREEN LINNET SIF 3012)

An excellent, lighthearted album that features Gerry O'Beirne and Donal Lunny along with O'Connor. O'Connor's energy and technique seem boundless, and anyone who likes Irish music is sure to enjoy this one.

Fretted Instruments

Although there are records showing that the tenor banjo was played in Ireland as long as 90 years ago, fretted instruments in general are fairly recent entrants into the traditional music scene, and as a consequence, there really are no traditional ways of playing them. Largely by way of the British and American revivals, however, fretted instruments have been edging their way into the Irish scene, until today, they are an accepted part of Irish folk music. Foremost among these, of course, is the guitar, used in Ireland, as elsewhere, to accompany singing and solo melody instruments. Although guitar was used on some of Michael Coleman's records, it did not become prominent until the 1960s, when the popular Clancy Brothers caused it to be linked with Irish music in a lot of people's minds. Among the leading Irish guitarists today are Andy

McGlynn, Paul Brady, and Mícheál Ó Domhnaill, the latter two both fine singers as well. There is a feeling in some quarters, however, that the guitar is not ideally suited to playing Irish music since it is tuned in fourths and most Irish music is oriented toward fifths.

From Greece has come the bouzouki, a double-strung instrument similar to the cittern. Johnny Moynihan brought it to Irish music in the 1960s, when he was a member of the influential group Sweeney's Men. The best-known bouzouki player in Ireland today, however, is probably Donal Lunny, the prime mover behind both Planxty and the Bothy Band. Lunny uses the instrument to good effect in a variety of situations, primarily as accompaniment.

The mandolin and tenor (4-string) banjo likewise are being used extensively in Irish folk music today, primarily in bands. The mandolin has been used since the turn of the century but only recently has it been gaining wider favor, as has the tenor banjo, which was first brought to Ireland through traveling minstrel shows about 100 years ago.

Mick Moloney

Probably the leading exponent of fretted instruments in Irish traditional music is folklorist, scholar, record producer, musician, and performer Mick Moloney. Moloney was born in County Limerick, and although there was little traditional music around the area, there was music in his home. He began guitar lessons at the age of 15, but it was the skiffle movement that got him interested in folk music, and through the music of the Clancy Brothers, he was directed back to Irish music and the more authentic traditional songs that were at the root of the Clancy Brothers' material.

Moloney attended University College in Dublin but spent weekends in neighboring County Clare, where traditional musicians were plentiful. He worked his way through college playing in a trio with two friends, one of whom was Donal Lunny. The group disbanded, and he continued in graduate school, but he and roommate Paul Brady played regularly in Dublin's traditional music circles.

Eventually Moloney was asked to join the Johnstons, a popular group that played folk and contemporary music, and in time Paul Brady also joined the fold. In 1971 Moloney left the group and went to Norway, then to London, where he worked as a social worker and also played the clubs.

Since 1973 Moloney has been associated with the folklore department at the University of Pennsylvania and is a noted authority on Irish traditional music. He organizes concerts, does research, produces records, performs, and has served as a consultant on Irish music for organizations ranging from the Smithsonian Institution's Festival of American Folklife to Philadelphia's Folk Life Center.

Moloney is an accomplished guitarist and conversant with the bouzouki, but his work on banjo and mandolin outshines the rest. He plays rapidly and precisely, embellishing the tunes with many of the ornaments associated with other instruments, at times a difficult feat. Because the banjo had not become established in the tradition when he began to play it, he had no role models and turned instead to musicians on other instruments as examples.

Moloney's musical interests are not limited to instrumental music, nor are they restricted to Ireland alone. He is a fine singer, and his repertoire includes songs from England and Scotland as well as Scandinavia. He has said that his aim is to promote greater acceptance of the banjo and mandolin in Irish traditional music, and toward this goal, he has recorded the first album devoted solely to Irish traditional tunes played on the banjo and mandolin.

S·E·L·E·C·T·E·D R·E·C·O·R·D·I·N·G·S

Mick Moloney with Eugene O'Donnell
(GREEN LINNET SIF 1010)
•
Strings Attached
(GREEN LINNET SIF 1027)

In a way, the first album is a showcase for Moloney's many talents, for it includes songs as well as tunes and features Moloney on a variety of instruments. He is joined by an assortment of outstanding musicians, and the album is further enhanced by extensive liner notes. *Strings Attached* is Moloney's long-awaited solo instrumental album featuring Irish traditional music on banjo and mandolin, with guitar and bouzouki overdubbed. It is of particular interest to aficionados of fretted instruments.

The Singing Tradition

For many people the Clancy Brothers immediately come to mind whenever Irish traditional singing is mentioned. Yet that particular brand of music, while influential in attracting converts to the folk fold, can scarcely be considered traditional. There are, in fact, a number of facets to the Irish vocal tradition, both in English and Irish, and few have anything to do with the commercialization of Irish song. Like the instrumental tradition, Irish song is solo and unaccompanied, with regional variations in style, and more highly ornamented than either English or Scots.

Probably the oldest singing tradition still vital in Ireland owes a debt to the ancient bardic tradition. Called *sean-nós* or old-style singing, it is highly ornamented, unaccompanied, and sung in Irish. Sean-nós songs tend to be lyrical rather than narrative in subject matter; that quality makes them more suitable for the elaborate ornamentation that is the sean-nós singer's trademark because there is no story to advance. The style requires great skill, but it cannot be compared with European singing traditions, for it is an entity unto itself. The sean-nós singer doesn't convey emotions through dynamics of loud and soft, as a European singer would, but rather through use of ornamentation—or lack of it. Another characteristic of sean-nós singing is melodic and rhythmic variation; the singer will not sing any two verses in a song in the same way and must be something of a composer as well.

Like sean-nós singing, other Irish-language vocal traditions tend to be concentrated in the Gaeltacht regions. These, however, are generally less mannered and usually deal with the concerns of everyday life.

The Irish- and English-language traditions in Ireland are not entirely distinct, however. There are songs that combine the languages, perhaps evidence of the transition from Irish to English as the national tongue. These songs will often alternate verses in each language, or have the verses in English and the chorus in Irish.

In either language, songs dealing with the subject of love predominate. As English came to be increasingly widely adopted, however, Anglo influences came to play as well. Songs in English can be roughly divided into two categories: English and Scots songs and Anglo-Irish songs. English and Scots songs are those that originated in England or Scotland and for a variety of reasons found their way into Ireland, through people traveling between the countries and through printed broadsides. Anglo-Irish songs are those that originated in Ireland, in the English language. Although love songs were the most common type, native Irish songs in English also included their share of songs dealing with disasters, murders, and executions—the favorite province of the broadsides. Any political movement was served by its own songs, and songs about the struggle for independence were particularly visible.

Packie Byrne, Sarah Makem, Margaret Barry, Paddy Tunney, and Joe Heaney are among the leading singers of the older generation. And through the folk revivals, younger Irish singers are taking the native singing traditions and often adding accompaniment. While their musical origins are unmistakably Irish, they are adapting the tradition for modern sensibilities, often successfully, other times less so, depending on the skill and sensitivity of the musicians involved.

Joe Heaney

Joe Heaney is widely acclaimed as one of the finest Irish singers. A practitioner of sean-nós singing, he sings both in English and in Irish, although he favors the latter because it was his first language, and he is more comfortable with it.

Heaney was born in 1920 in West Connemara. His father was a singer, and singing was so fully integrated into his daily life that Heaney cannot fix a time to when he began singing himself.

PHOTO BY MARK MAMALAKIS

*Joe Heaney has lived in the United
States since the early 1960s
but remains one of the finest Irish
traditional singers in the world.*

Heaney left Connemara in 1940, at the age of 20, and went to Dublin to sing at the Feis Ceoil, winning first prize in the singing competition. Between 1949 and 1957 he lived in England, and in the early 1960s he emigrated to the US.

Since settling in the US, Heaney has made a name for himself not only as a fine singer but as a link to centuries of Irish traditional music. He is acutely aware of the fact that he is carrying on something precious and is well informed about the class history that has shaped his life (he has earned his living as a laborer and doorman). He has played at colleges and festivals all over the US, and returns regularly to his homeland, where he remains a highly respected figure.

Heaney's singing, both in Irish and in English, is restrained, highly ornamented, and entirely unaccompanied, rooted in his sense of tradition, history, and culture. He is a storyteller as well as a singer, and as living evidence of the continuity of the Irish tradition, he has long been bridging the gap between the older traditions and modern life.

S·E·L·E·C·T·E·D R·E·C·O·R·D·I·N·G·S

Joe Heaney
(PHILO 2004)
•
With Gabe O'Sullivan:
Joe and the Gabe
(GREEN LINNET SIF 1018)

The Philo release features Heaney exclusively, singing unaccompanied in both Irish and English. The Green Linnet album features whistle player Gabe O'Sullivan as well. The tone of this record is not so much a collaboration as that of an informal "session," as each cut is a solo performance, much as it would be at such a gathering. For that reason, as well as the variety, it is probably easier to listen to and more enjoyable than the Philo release, which will most likely appeal to those specifically interested in Irish culture and tradition.

Paddy Tunney

Although born in Glasgow in 1921, Paddy Tunney was brought up in Ireland, his family's home. His childhood was marked by a great deal of music; not only was his mother Brigid a well-known source singer, whose songs were collected by Peter Kennedy for the BBC, but Tunney himself has been singing since he was four years old, and absorbed much of his mother's considerable repertoire.

After attending technical school, Tunney went to work as a forester for the Ministry of Agriculture in Northern Ireland. In 1941 he joined the IRA, teaching Irish history on the sly and holding drills in fields at night. In 1942 he took a job as a road-roller flagman and became part of the counter-espionage force of the IRA. In 1943, while carrying explosives on a bus, he was stopped, searched, and arrested. In the ensuing trial he was found guilty of possessing explosives with intent to damage life or property, and served 4½ years of a seven-year sentence.

Tunney's singing provides much the same link with tradition that Joe Heaney's does. His style, like Heaney's, is intricately but subtly ornamented, but he is probably more accessible to the modern ear than Heaney is. His singing has clear ties to the instrumental tradition, employing runs, stops, grace notes, and so on, much like pipe and fiddle music, and in addition to being a renowned singer, Tunney is a champion lilter. He has collected songs from all over Ireland and has sung for Radio Eireann and the BBC, as well as appearing at local festivals.

S·E·L·E·C·T·E·D   R·E·C·O·R·D·I·N·G·S

The Mountain Streams Where the Moorcocks Crow
(TOPIC 12TS264)

•

The Man of Songs
(FOLK-LEGACY FSE-1)

•

The Stone Fiddle
(GREEN LINNET SIF 1037)

Of these records, all of which are very good, the Folk-Legacy release stands out, mainly because Tunney seems not only to have more energy than on the others but to be in very fine voice as well. This isn't too surprising, considering the fact that it was recorded in 1962, when he was still fairly young. The years seem to have taken their toll on his voice, and *The Stone Fiddle* in particular, recorded 20 years later than the Folk-Legacy album, seems to show the strain. Both the Topic and the Folk-Legacy records include examples of his lilting, but any one of these albums is a fine example of the singing of one of Ireland's best traditional singers.

Andy Irvine

Although Andy Irvine gained most of his notoriety as a member of the original and re-formed Planxty, he has been highly visible as a solo performer as well. A fan of Woody Guthrie, Jack Elliott, and Derroll Adams, Irvine was a part of the so-called ballad revival in Dublin in the early 1960s.

In the middle of the decade, Irvine formed a group called Sweeney's Men, with Terry Woods and Joe Dolan. When Woods left, Johnny Moynihan stepped in, and the group was highly influential although not enormously successful.

Irvine left Sweeney's Men before the band's second record and traveled extensively in Eastern Europe, especially Bulgaria, Romania, and Yugoslavia, developing an affinity for Balkan music. After returning to Ireland, Irvine participated in Christy Moore's *Prosperous* session and subsequently joined Planxty. When the band broke up in the mid-1970s, Irvine paired up with Paul Brady, Planxty's last lead singer, making an album with him and touring America before parting company two years later. When Planxty re-formed late in the decade, Irvine once again was a member.

Irvine is a singer, songwriter, and multi-instrumentalist, whose musical expertise includes proficiency on mandola, bouzouki, hurdy-gurdy, harmonica and guitar. Like Christy Moore's, Irvine's approach to music is low-key, and tends to be highly arranged, but he is a stronger singer, somewhat gentle and caressing in his style. His music clearly reflects his interest in Balkan music—he often includes Balkan songs, and has adapted the rhythms in other material. He also uses jazz-inspired chords in some of his accompaniments. His instrumental work is most accomplished and energetic, and he is one of the best of the younger musicians in Ireland.

S·E·L·E·C·T·E·D R·E·C·O·R·D·I·N·G

Rainy Sundays . . . Windy Dreams
(TARA 3002)

Joined by Donal Lunny, Paul Brady, and Liam O'Flynn, Irvine has produced an enjoyable record. The first side is dominated by the three-part "The Emigrants," a trio of songs all dealing with the problem of Irish emigration to America. Side 2 includes a couple of Balkan songs and tunes; juxtaposed with Irvine's other music, the pervasive Eastern influence becomes more readily apparent. Highly recommended.

Boys of the Lough

The Boys of the Lough aren't strictly Irish—or Scottish or English, for that matter. While other bands generally stick to the music of their own country, the Boys take a more international approach, playing music from Scotland, Ireland, and the Shetland Isles. Yet the focus is clearly Celtic, and the Boys of the Lough were the first Celtic band to work on an exclusively professional basis.

The Boys have enjoyed some of the leading figures of the folk scene as members of the group. An early member was Dick Gaughan; another ex-member is Robin Morton, now running Temple Records. The core of the group has always been Shetland fiddler Aly Bain, whose incomparable playing stands as some of the best on the folk scene in any country, and Cathal McConnell, an Irish whistle and flute player and singer par excellence. The current configuration includes Dave Richardson on fretted instruments and concertina, and his brother Tich, who replaced Robin Morton and plays guitar.

The Boys of the Lough came together in the early 1970s, the merger of two duos—Mike Whellans and Aly Bain, and Cathal McConnell and Robin Morton. Whellans left before the group's first album was completed, and Dick Gaughan stepped into his shoes, although he too left after the album was completed. Dave Richardson came in upon Gaughan's departure.

While the music of other Celtic or Irish bands may be lively and well played, that of the Boys of the Lough is in a class by itself. Although very tight musically, the Boys nonetheless manage to convey a sense of great fun and excitement; they are, in short, irresistible, and tremendously popular in the US as well as Britain and Ireland.

Despite the change in personnel, McConnell's whistle and flute and Bain's fiddle playing continue to be the focus of the music. Tich Richardson tends to slip a few jazz chords in now and then, which gives the music an altogether different character than it had while Morton was a member of the band, but Morton's banjo and bodhran playing contributed a rhythmic backdrop that, if not indispensable, was an integral and satisfying part of their sound. The extra ounce of vitality he added will be sorely missed, and the lineup that included him probably marked the Boys' finest hour.

S·E·L·E·C·T·E·D R·E·C·O·R·D·I·N·G·S

Second Album
(ROUNDER 3006)
·
Lochaber No More
(PHILO 1031)
·
The Piper's Broken Finger
(PHILO PH 1042)

Three fine albums from the incarnation of the band that included Dave Richardson and Robin Morton. All reflect vigorous instrumentals and excellent vocals, and *The Piper's Broken Finger* features the addition of Highland bagpipes on a few cuts. Virtually any of the Boys' albums would be a sound musical investment.

Planxty

One of the most highly acclaimed and most popular of the Irish groups, Planxty was largely the offshoot of Christy Moore's album *Prosperous*. The original members of the band all had played on the album and had enjoyed playing together so much, they decided to remain together as a group. They released a single, "The Cliffs of Dooneen," which proved highly successful on the Irish charts, and Planxty was signed to an exclusive recording contract as a result. The original lineup included Moore, Donal Lunny, Andy Irvine, and Liam Og O'Flynn. Lunny left after two albums and was replaced with Johnny Moynihan, on his way to De Danann. Moore then left, and Paul Brady took his place until the group disbanded, shortly thereafter. The members went their separate ways until late in the 1970s, when the group re-formed. Matt Molloy was a member for a short time, before he left to join the Chieftains, but with his departure, Planxty was back to its original lineup. More recently, the band has incorporated a fiddler and a synthesizer player.

Along with the Chieftains, Planxty has been the primary group responsible for exposing traditional Irish music to a wider audience. Of course, the influence of the British revival is evident in their approach; despite O'Flynn's presence, they make extensive use of guitar, lending their music a distinctly modern sound, but their roots are unmistakably in the Irish tradition. Andy Irvine's Balkan songs have crept onto on album or two, and Liam O'Flynn's pipes are highly distinctive, but the band also has a group identity, and chances are, you wouldn't mistake their music for anyone else's. At times they can be uneven, despite the undeniable talent of the members; but individually and collectively the members of Planxty remain among the foremost figures of the Irish folk scene.

S·E·L·E·C·T·E·D R·E·C·O·R·D·I·N·G·S

Planxty
(POLYDOR SUPER 2383 186; SHANACHIE 79009)
•
The Well Below the Valley
(POLYDOR SUPER 2383 232; SHANACHIE 79010)

The band's first two efforts remain its best, despite the release of several more since. *The Well Below the Valley* is particularly worthy of note. Both records point up the strengths and weaknesses of the band, however; although each member clearly is an excellent musician, there is a certain fragmented feeling at times, with a corresponding sense that sometimes they took the easy way out when arranging their music. One also might wish for a little more conviction behind the vocals.

The Bothy Band

The Bothy Band was fairly short-lived, but from 1975 to 1979 they were a major force in folk music, and their influence persists even now, years since their dissolution.

The original Bothy Band was made up of fiddle player Tommy Peoples, Donal Lunny on guitar, bodhran, and bouzouki; Paddy Keenan on pipes; Matt Molloy on flute and whistle; and siblings Tríona Ní Dhomhnaill and Mícheál Ó Domhnaill on vocals, and clavinet, and guitar, respectively. Peoples left after their first album and was replaced by Kevin Burke, whose fiddle style was softer and more ornamented, and, in turn, made their music gentler, but no less compelling. Their instrumentation was a curious mix of the modern and the traditional and they clearly owed a debt to rock as well as traditional music. The pipes, flute, whistle, and fiddle formed the melody section, while the guitars, bouzouki, clavinet, and bodhran formed the rhythm section. A remarkable dynamic existed between the rich sound of their full arrangements and the delicacy of their solos.

But their vocal strengths, too, were considerable. Although the Bothy Band was primarily an instrumental group, the Ó Domhnaills had a rich source of song in their aunt Neili, and they availed themselves of the material for some remarkably fine singing. Tríona's jewellike voice lent a warmth and purity to their sound, while Mícheál's approach was gentler, at times almost retiring. Many of the songs they sang were in Irish.

The Bothy Band had a big sound, at once driving and joyous, lighthearted and intense and, occasionally, deeply affecting. Theirs was an expansive music; it reached out to embrace the listener, then wouldn't let him go.

S·E·L·E·C·T·E·D R·E·C·O·R·D·I·N·G·S

1975
(MULLIGAN LUN 002)
•
Old Hag You Have Killed Me
(MULLIGAN LUN 007; GREEN LINNET SIF 3005)
•
The Best of the Bothy Band
(MULLIGAN LUN 041; GREEN LINNET SIF 3001)

While *1975* and *Old Hag You Have Killed Me* are instructive in terms of the change that took place with Tommy Peoples' departure and Kevin Burke's appearance in the group, each is a superb recording in its own right. Particularly memorable are "Calum Sgaire" and "Fionnghuala" on *Old Hag,* the latter an exhilarating rush of Scottish mouth music. The *Best of* record shows the full range of the group, from start to finish, with highlights of the band's recording career. Included are live as well as studio performances, and "Casadh An tSugain" is positively riveting.

De Danann

Fretted instruments abound in De Danann, a group originally composed of Dolores Keane, Frankie Gavin on fiddle and flute, Charlie Piggot on banjo, Alec Finn on bouzouki and guitar, and Johnny "Ringo" McDonagh on bodhran and bones. Keane left after the band's first album, to be replaced by Johnny Moynihan. When Moynihan left, Tim Lyons came in his stead and, more recently, Jackie Daly, who is a superb accordion player. Daly has recently departed from the group, however, and Mary Bergin has been part of the lineup.

De Danann came together in the mid-1970s and quickly gained considerable popularity. Although they are extremely smooth musically, their most outstanding trait may very well be their willingness to experiment. On their third album, *The Mist Covered Mountain,* they included two traditional singers along with instrumental accompaniment. Their fourth album, furthermore, featured their rendition of "Hey Jude," arranged in a distinctly Irish manner.

De Danann's music is highly rhythmic, a feature that is augmented by McDonagh's vigorous bodhran playing, which sets off the other instruments. Their instrumentals make up in polish for what they occasionally lack in punch, but overall the band is one of the slickest on the Irish scene. They were stronger vocally when Keane was part of the group, but with the addition of Maura O'Connell on their fourth album, they seemed to be regaining some of their old ground. Unfortunately, she is no longer with the group.

S·E·L·E·C·T·E·D R·E·C·O·R·D·I·N·G·S

De Danann
(BOOT ITB 4018)
•
Selected Jigs, Reels and Songs
(DECCA (UK) SKLR 5287)
•
The Mist Covered Mountain
(SHANACHIE 79005)
•
The Star Spangled Molly
(OGHAM 5005; SHANACHIE 79018)

De Danann features the singing of Dolores Keane, as well as the buoyant instrumentals the group is known for; if only there was more of her singing! *Selected Jigs, Reels and Songs* marks Johnny Moynihan's entry into the band and contains some of the best instrumental work they have done. *The Mist Covered Mountain* likewise is strong instrumentally but is unique in its inclusion of traditional singers along with instrumental accompaniment—a combination that works surprisingly well. *The Star Spangled Molly* is a nostalgic collection of songs and tunes that pay homage to the Irish-American music of the 1920s and features Maura O'Connell on vocals; don't miss its novelty track—"Hey Jude."

Clannad

Clannad has been described by some as an Irish Pentangle, and while that does go a way toward describing their sound, it doesn't really give the group adequate credit for their enormous creativity. For Clannad's music is a unique merger of traditional, classical, and especially jazz influences, and their sound is exclusively their own.

Clannad is comprised of Máire Ní Bhraonáin, Ciaran and Pól Ó Braonáin and their uncles Noel and Padraig Ó Dúgain; on their sixth album they were joined by Eithne Ni Bhraonain. Individually, the members don't always impress; their work on fretted instruments for example, is easily surpassed by that of other musicians. But the blend of the parts is stunning, and Máire's harp, Pól's flute and whistle, and Ciaran's bass are all remarkably fresh. Vocally, too, they are strong, especially Máire, and Clannad excels at both songs and tunes, making a concerted effort to avoid material that has been played to death.

Clannad was formed in 1969–70 and won their first recording contract as first prize in a festival they entered. Their music is shaped by the fact that they are from the Donegal Gaeltacht and sing almost exclusively in Irish. And they don't feel influenced by other groups. As they explained it, "We started to appreciate all the songs from our area [but] when we got into a room and decided to stick chords onto them, they were just contemporary things too." They also added amplification, although retaining acoustic instruments.

They cull their material from a variety of sources, concentrating on the music from their own area. Some of it they have known since childhood; some they get from books or from the old people in their area. When they first began playing, it was not fashionable to sing songs in Irish, but they were determined not to compromise and continued playing the music they wanted to play in the way they wanted to play it. In time they grew to tremendous popularity in Britain, Ireland, and Europe and completed a successful tour of the United States in 1979.

S·E·L·E·C·T·E·D R·E·C·O·R·D·I·N·G·S

Dulaman
(SHANACHIE 79008)
•
Clannad in Concert
(OGHAM BLB 5001)
•
Fuaim
(TARA 3008)

Each of these records presents a different facet of Clannad's music. The first, the group's third effort, is a fine studio album, highlighted by the rendering of "Two Sisters," a well-known Child ballad; "Siuil a Run"; and a number of fine instrumentals. The concert album is probably their best effort to date, and a standout among live albums in general; there isn't a bad or even mediocre cut on it, capped by "Níl sên lá," a ten-minute song interrupted in the middle by dynamic solo improvisations. _Fuaim_ is the band's sixth album, and on it they are joined by Eithne Ni Bhraonain, as well as studio musicians playing electric guitar, clarinet, saxophone, and drums. It is their most strongly jazz-flavored record, and one wishes for more harp, but the collective vocals and instrumentals are a treat.

Paul Brady

There can scarcely be a finer singer in Ireland than Paul Brady. Riddled with tension lying just under the surface, his music has an explosive quality that invariably leaves an enormous impression on the listener.

Brady hails from County Tyrone. His parents were singers, and all his life he has been exposed to music, from Irish traditional songs and tunes to jazz and rock. His musical career was under way by the time he was 16, during the early 1960s, when he played piano at a hotel in Donegal, and his career since has been marked by participation in two influential groups—the Johnstons and Planxty. It is Brady's solo work, however, that is the most compelling. He is a singer of remarkable strength and power, and this despite a delivery that at times may seem understated and very controlled.

Brady is almost as well known for his instrumental work as for his singing, and his name is frequently found among the credits on records of Irish music. He is a first-rate guitarist, with a distinctive syncopated style; an excellent piano player and whistle player; and proficient on a number of other instruments, including mandolin and bouzouki.

Brady's stint with the Johnstons, a folk-oriented contemporary group, ended in 1976, and he returned from North America, where he had been playing, to join Planxty. When the band split, he and Andy Irvine performed together for a couple of years. Their work was highly acclaimed, and Brady went on to record a solo album, *Welcome Here Kind Stranger*, which was named *Melody Maker*'s folk album of the year in 1978. Aside from an album of Sean O'Casey's poems, however, which he arranged and, in many cases, set to music, Brady's more recent efforts have been focused on contemporary rock and songwriting, culminating in the release of an album, *Hard Station*.

Brady sings in a highly ornamented style, in a clear, penetrating tenor that forces the listener to sit up and take notice. He truly eclipses all his peers. Now, if only he'd record more!

S·E·L·E·C·T·E·D R·E·C·O·R·D·I·N·G·S

Andy Irvine/Paul Brady
(MULLIGAN LUN 008; GREEN LINNET SIF 3006)
•
Welcome Here Kind Stranger
(MULLIGAN LUN 024; GREEN LINNET SIF 3015)

Although Brady has appeared as an instrumentalist on many albums, these, which feature his singing, remain his best. *Andy Irvine/Paul Brady* is an excellent album, with Brady's version of "Arthur McBride" particularly noteworthy; Irvine's contributions are also very good, but Brady, as usual, comes out supreme. *Welcome Here Kind Stranger* is the kind of album that grows—and grows and grows—on you. It is a superlative achievement from start to finish.

Dolores Keane

Dolores Keane may not always be as visible as other singers, but it's not because she isn't as good. On the contrary, she is exceptional—possibly the best female singer in Ireland, with an understated but radiant approach to her music.

A member of a well-known musical family—her aunts Sarah and Rita Keane are traditional singers specializing in unison singing—Keane herself was the original singer with the band De Danann, although she left after the group's first album. She also sang on the Chieftains' album *Bonaparte's Retreat*. More recently, she has been singing with her husband John Faulkner, who was a member of Ewan MacColl's Critics Group, and a group called the Reel Union.

Keane and Company perform music from Scotland and England as well as Ireland, a multinational approach that is undoubtedly a reflection of Faulkner's English origins and Keane's Irish ones. The result is superb music arranged and played with consummate taste and acute sensitivity, among the finest being produced today.

Keane also plays whistle and concertina, but her low voice

is what immediately commands attention; it is positively stunning, with a burnished quality, at once substantial and luminous. She exercises complete control over her vocal chords, impressing with subtlety rather than showiness, all the while managing to convey the kind of tension that is essential for good music.

If you can buy the records of only two Irish singers, make Dolores Keane's one of them (and Paul Brady's the other).

S·E·L·E·C·T·E·D R·E·C·O·R·D·I·N·G·S

With John Faulkner and Eamonn Curran:
Farewell to Eirinn
(GREEN LINNET SIF 3003)

·

With John Faulkner and The Reel Union:
Broken-Hearted I'll Wander
(MULLIGAN LUN 033; GREEN LINNET SIF 3004)

Two exquisite records for quiet listening. While each has its share of lively instrumentals, the high points are, of course, Keane's singing, although Faulkner's is awfully good too.

Tríona Ní Dhomhnaill

Tríona Ní Dhomhnaill's voice is as ethereal as Dolores Keane's is substantial. Gifted with a marvelously clear soprano, she weaves a musical spell, often singing the songs of her aunt Neili, a source singer who contributed 286 songs to the University College, Dublin's folklore collection.

Like Dolores Keane, Tríona is a member of a musical family; in addition to her aunt, both her sister Mairead and brother Mícheál are singers, and she and her siblings were members of a short-lived group called Skara Brae. Tríona is probably best known, however, as a member of the Bothy Band, which integrated jazz, rock, and other contemporary influences into traditional Irish music.

Tríona sings in both Irish and English and plays keyboard instruments, including the clavinet, an instrument that sounds like a small harpsichord. Her voice is light and sylph-like; yet despite the delicate character of her music, Tríona Ní Dhomhnaill is a potent musician. Her voice soaring into a song, she holds her listener hostage long after the music has ended.

After the demise of the Bothy Band, Tríona came to the US. She now has settled in North Carolina, where she has a new band.

S·E·L·E·C·T·E·D R·E·C·O·R·D·I·N·G·S

Tríona
(GAEL-LINN CEF 043)

·

With Touchstone:
The New Land
(GREEN LINNET SIF 1040)

The solo album on Gael-Linn clearly is the superior record, mainly because it features more of Tríona, joined by some of Ireland's best musicians. Its strong point is, of course, its vocals, both accompanied and unaccompanied. The solitary instrumental demonstrates her proficiency on the clavinet and is most pleasing. *Touchstone* is a pleasant enough album but marred by the very thing that is *Tríona*'s strength—there's not enough Tríona. The other musicians are all very good, at least instrumentally, but the other female member of the group in no way can be classed with Tríona as a singer, and it seems a shame not to have used the space for more of Tríona. Still, if you're a fan of Tríona, converted or incipient, you'll want it in your record collection anyway.

Groups

Because the Irish tradition is essentially solo and unaccompanied, musical groups are a fairly recent phenomenon. There is a tradition of sorts associated with the large ceilí bands that grew to prominence during the 1920s—groups of 8 or 9 musicians playing in unison on fiddles, flutes, and accordions. In time, however, piano, drums, double bass, saxophones, guitars, and banjo were added, something more in common with the swing bands than the Irish tradition.

Although the ceilí bands were popular, they were deplored by many, not the least of whom was Seán Ó Riada, a composer, teacher, and music director who responded to the ceilí bands by forming the Ceoltoiri Chualann, a group composed of musicians playing traditional music on traditional instruments in structured arrangements that complemented the music. Out of the Ceoltoiri Chualann grew the Chieftains, a band founded on similar principles and derived from Ceoltoiri Chualann membership. The Chieftains achieved a position of considerable prominence, and the tastefulness and vigor of their music established a new pattern for group playing of traditional Irish music, paving the way for such bands as Planxty, the Bothy Band, and De Danann, which sprang up during the 1960s.

The British revival also contributed to the formation of Irish bands. Drawing on the success of groups like Steeleye Span in the early 1970s, the new Irish bands began to take form, freely adding instruments like the bouzouki and the clavinet to the traditional instruments that dominated the lineups. One particularly influential band of the 1960s, Sweeney's Men, enjoyed only moderate success during its career but pioneered the use of counterpoint and cross-rhythms, which in turn found their way into the music of later groups. With such well-known figures as Andy Irvine and Johnny Moynihan in their ranks, Sweeney's Men also employed amplification for a brief period. The result of such experimentation was freer interpretation of traditional music, and it has contributed mightily to the development of marvelously inventive and multidimensional music that speaks to the modern ear as well as to the tradition.

The Chieftains

They first burst into the public consciousness as the band that did the soundtrack for the movie _Barry Lyndon,_ but the Chieftains actually had been around a lot longer than that. A group of highly accomplished musicians noted for their elegant and lush arrangements of traditional Irish music, they are among the best-known and -loved groups in the world.

The Chieftains formed in the early 1960s; the core of the group was associated with Seán Ó Riada's Ceoltoiri Chualann but wanted to pursue their own musical interests while remaining in Ó Riada's group. The shared members continued to balance their commitments to both groups until Ceoltoiri Chualann disbanded, at which point they devoted their full attention to the Chieftains.

The Chieftains center around Paddy Moloney, one of the foremost pipers in the world, and he generally serves as the band's spokesman and musical director. It was he who began to guide the group more toward creative interpretation in the early 1970s, and their repertoire since has included original compositions as well as traditional tunes. Another of the band's most visible members is harper Derek Bell. Bell, who is a classically trained musician, joined the Chieftains around the time of their fourth album. Although gut-strung harps are more common in Irish music, they are not really traditional, and Bell plays a metal-strung harp as well as a gut-strung one in deference to the ancient Irish harp tradition. Other long-time members of the group include Martin Fay, Sean Keane on fiddle, and, more recently, Matt Molloy.

The Chieftains' sound is wonderfully rich—almost orchestral—but at the same time airy and exuberant. Their material tends to be highly melodic, and although it clearly is arranged, it sacrifices none of its vitality.

The Chieftains themselves have sometimes been criticized for being overly dry and academic in their approach to their music, but that's largely a matter of interpretation. What remains indisputable is that they have interested a huge international audience in the traditional music of Ireland and, in the process, maintained their musical integrity.

S·E·L·E·C·T·E·D R·E·C·O·R·D·I·N·G

The Chieftains 5
(ISLAND ILPS 9334)

A fair sampling of the Chieftains' music and thoroughly enjoyable. It's hard to pick one or two cuts as outshining the others—they're all excellent—but a medley of O'Carolan tunes is especially beautiful, and the Kerry slides that wind the record up are sheer delight, from the group's lilting to Bell's ethereal harp and Moloney's elegant piping. It's worth noting, however, that the Chieftains are better live than on record—a view that apparently is not shared by their record company, as they currently have about 10 albums available.

UNITED STATES
The Mountain Tradition

For many years academics viewed the thriving tradition of the Appalachian Mountains as a quaint but insignificant carryover from older, simpler times. Admittedly, some of the archaic ballads that the people seemed so fond of might have some literary value, but the singing tradition itself was of little or no consequence.

With the early years of this century, however, the musical traditions of America slowly began to receive the recognition they deserved. In 1910 John A. Lomax, later head of the Archive of Folk Song at the Library of Congress, published his influential *Cowboy Songs and Other Frontier Ballads,* and soon other, smaller collections of folk songs began to appear. Between 1916 and 1918 celebrated English folklorist Cecil Sharp made a field trip to the United States, and in 1919 published his *English Folk Songs from the Southern Appalachians,* identifying the Appalachians as a treasure trove of traditional music. Other folklorists followed suit, locating sources of British traditional music all over the country, from New England to the Southwest.

Not all the songs that were collected were traceable to British ballads, of course. Folk music in America served the same function as it had in Britain, and the people who settled the United States not only adapted the old songs to fit their new environment but created new songs as well. Songs of knights, kings, and princesses might have been in order in Britain, but in the fledgling country they had little place, and tales and songs documenting the exploits of local heroes moved in to take their place. Where songs in Britain had dealt with the supernatural, their American counterparts tended to diminish those elements. Universal themes persisted—love and betrayal remained the most common—but in America, murder ballads attained positions of particular prominence. As in Britain, work songs were a major part of the common pool, but in a country as vast as the US, just beginning to expand and develop, songs about the frontier and, in time, the railroad that made it accessible, became just as important. The Industrial Revolution and its effects made it into song, too, and the dismal conditions of the workers, particularly the miners, were fodder for a barrage of protest songs.

Singing styles changed too. While the old songs retained their modal melodies, and ballads continued to be sung unaccompanied, for the most part, the American way of singing was less ornamented than the British or Irish.

A major force in early folk music was religion. Not only does religious content permeate traditional American song, but the advent of harmony singing can be traced to the singing schools that flourished during the 17th and 18th centuries. These schools, which originated in New England, were the product of itinerant singing teachers who traveled the country from small town to small town, teaching the citizens part singing in a combination of secular and sacred influences. By the end of the 19th century, the characteristic "shape notes" had been invented to indicate the pitch of the notes for the musically illiterate, and by the early 1800s, such sacred harp (or "fasola" or shape note) singing had found its way south, where it has remained a vital tradition into the 20th century.

Harmony singing antedated the widespread introduction of musical instruments in the hills, both because the instruments were hard to obtain and because many denominations forbade them as part of their doctrine. But the early settlers carried with them the instrumental traditions of Britain—the jigs, reels, and country dances of their homeland. The fiddle was the leading instrument used at country dances and undoubtedly entered the mountains with the first settlers. Many fiddle tunes originated in Britain; others were of American composition. The dulcimer, a simple, quiet instrument that was held in the lap and strummed or picked, was popular in some areas, particularly Kentucky. The banjo, now inextricably linked with old-time mountain music, originated with the black population and most likely was derived from an African prototype. It didn't gain favor in the southern mountains until the late 19th century, around the same time the guitar was finding acceptance; the mandolin became popular early in the 20th century.

Ethnic musical styles also affected the developing white southern style. Mexican sources from the Southwest introduced the guitar, and in Louisiana Cajun fiddle styles proved influential. The musical exchange between black and white musicians undoubtedly was the strongest influence, though, contributing not only many songs but rhythms, and the entire notion of instrumentation that considered the accompanying instrument as important as the voice in a song. Many guitar styles are traceable to black musical styles, and many musicians picked up blues inflections. Traveling medicine shows further established instruments in an accompanying role to song.

The growth of mass communications in this century, coupled with the shifting of population to the cities, has tended to blur the stylistic differences that existed in the mountains and diminished the tradition somewhat. Through the efforts of such folklorists as John and Alan Lomax, Kenneth Goldstein, and numerous others, however, the music of many traditional singers and instrumentalists has been preserved, both on record and in the Archive of Folk Culture at the Library of Congress. The folk revival has performed an additional service over the years in focusing attention on the traditional performers and bringing many of them to prominence, where audiences familiar with the music of folk song interpreters can hear and enjoy the sources who have kept alive the musical traditions themselves.

S·E·L·E·C·T·E·D R·E·C·O·R·D·I·N·G·S

Anthology of American Folk Music, Volumes 1–3
(FOLKWAYS FA 2951-3)
•
Folk Music in America
(15 Volumes)
(LIBRARY OF CONGRESS LBC 1–15)

These are probably the two foremost anthologies of traditional American music. The Folkways set, six records, is organized into ballads; social music, including religious music; and songs, and includes music from a variety of traditions, black and white. It was edited by Harry Smith and taken from his extensive record collection. The music included was recorded commercially between 1927 and 1932. The Library of Congress set, produced to commemmorate the American Bicentennial, was edited by Richard K. Spottswood and includes material from the Library of Congress archives. Virtually every ethnic tradition you can think of is represented, and detailed notes and excellent production make this one of the most important projects of recorded traditional music in the US.

Jean Ritchie

No other musician has bridged the gap between tradition and revival more successfully than Jean Ritchie. The youngest of 14 children, Jean was raised in Viper, Kentucky, a region as rich in the musical traditions of the Scottish-Irish-English people who originally settled there as it was in natural resources.

Scholarly interest in the Ritchie family began before Jean was born. In 1917 Cecil Sharp visited the family and transcribed many songs from her father and other members of the family. In the 1930s, when Jean was a child, John and Alan Lomax recorded members of the family for the Library of Congress Archive of Folk Song.

The songs Jean learned as a child were not the popular "hillbilly" tunes of the day, but rather the ballads that her ancestors had brought with them across the Atlantic, along with newer ones. Leisuretime often meant the whole family would gather and sing.

Jean attended the University of Kentucky in Lexington, where she was awarded her bachelor's degree in social work in 1946. By mid-1947 she was working at the Henry Street Settlement in New York. She was also performing, and she met such key members of the folk revival as Pete Seeger, Leadbelly, Oscar Brand, Hobart Smith, and Brownie McGhee. During that time Alan Lomax also recorded her music for the Archive of Folk Song.

In 1952 Jean was awarded a Fulbright scholarship to study her family's origins in Britain. And in 1955 her book *Singing Family of the Cumberlands,* a history of her family, was published.

Straightforward and deceptively simple, Jean Ritchie's singing and accompaniments clearly are rooted in tradition. Her voice reflects a thin purity, accented by the traditional singer's decorations—quavers in the voice and embellishments to the melody line. Yet her fragile soprano captures infinite nuances and subtleties that bring the music alive.

And always it is the song itself that dominates. Much of her material continues to be the music she learned as a child, from children's play songs to the ballads. But equally affecting are the songs she has written herself. Most of these concern the land she grew up in, and many retain the modal melodies so characteristic of the traditional ballads of Appalachia.

More than anyone else, Jean Ritchie has been responsible for bringing to national attention the Appalachian, or mountain, dulcimer. And while many dulcimer players now play with greater complexity than she does, few can match her sensitivity. She also plays autoharp and guitar, but the dulcimer remains her primary instrument.

Jean Ritchie has been featured at folk festivals, folklore seminars, and at major universities. She has sung all over the US, Britain, and Europe. Yet it is not her fine scholarship that makes her stand out so much as the continuity her lovely singing provides with the past.

S·E·L·E·C·T·E·D R·E·C·O·R·D·I·N·G·S

British Traditional Ballads in the Southern Mountains, Volume 2
(FOLKWAYS FA 2302)
•
Clear Waters Remembered
(GEORDIE 101)
•
Jean Ritchie At Home
(PACIFIC CASCADE RECORDS LPL 7026)
•
Sweet Rivers
(JUNE APPAL JA 037)

This list could be much longer, as Jean Ritchie has been a prolific recording artist, but these albums represent various facets of her music. The first, as the title indicates, is a collection of Child ballads sung unaccompanied. *Clear Waters Remembered* includes some of her best-known original material, such as "Black Waters" and "Blue Diamond Mines." *Jean Ritchie at Home* is a lovely collection of songs, many traditional, with additions by Ritchie herself. *Sweet Rivers* is a collection of hymns, many unaccompanied, and illustrates the persistence of religious music in the tradition.

Frank Proffitt

In the late 1950s, when the Kingston Trio was enjoying un-precedented commercial success with their recording of "Tom Dooley," Frank Proffitt, the man from whom the song was collected, was struggling to provide his children with their school books. It is a bitter irony that Proffitt, who indirectly had an enormous impact on the folk boom of the 1950s and 1960s, never saw even a fraction of the riches that were made off his material.

Frank Proffitt was born in 1913 in Tennessee, but his family moved to North Carolina when he was a year old, and it was there that he spent the rest of his life. His childhood was filled with music, and he learned banjo making from his father, but hard times forced him to leave school after the sixth grade and go to work on his father's farm.

By the age of 20, Proffitt was married and the father of a child, and soon he was feeling the pinch of the Depression. Frequently during the 1930s he was forced to leave home to find work. Late in the decade he met collectors Frank and Anne Warner, who had asked Proffitt's father-in-law, Nathan Hicks, to make them a dulcimer. A friendship developed between the two families, and over the next 27 years the Warners collected over 120 songs from Proffitt.

In 1961, and for the few remaining years of his life, Proffitt finally was able to reap some of the acclaim due him. That year, he was invited to perform at the University of Chicago Folk Festival, and after that appearance offers not only poured in from all over the country, but he received numerous orders for his handmade fretless banjos and dulcimers. Proffitt's notoriety was short-lived, however, for he died tragically in November 1965, at the age of 52.

Perhaps because he was fairly young when he was re-corded, Frank Proffitt's music seems smoother than that of many traditional musicians. He had a warm, pleasing voice and a natural, unassuming delivery; his banjo and dulcimer playing were simple but effective and always appropriate to the songs. And he frequently adapted his instrumental tech-nique to evoke certain elements of the song, such as the whistle of a train. Although for an urban audience Frank Proffitt was probably one of the most accessible of the tradi-tional musicians, music clearly was a part of his daily life, and it had a depth that could only come from a personal musical heritage.

S·E·L·E·C·T·E·D R·E·C·O·R·D·I·N·G·S

Frank Proffitt Sings Folk Songs
(FOLKWAYS FA 2360)
•
Frank Proffitt
(FOLK-LEGACY FSA-1)

Both of these records present fine selections of Proffitt's songs, to banjo and dulcimer accompaniment. The Folk-Legacy record is a little slicker than the Folkways release, but not much, and both are excellent and highly enjoyable.

Hobart Smith

Although Hobart Smith was a first-rate singer, he is remembered primarily as one of the finest instrumentalists to come out of the American tradition, and he has remained a highly respected and revered figure long after his death in 1965.

Smith was born in 1897 in Virginia, one of 8 children. Both his parents played banjo, and Smith himself began playing the instrument at the age of 7; he picked up the fiddle and guitar in his teens. As an adult, he made his living in various ways, and played in a band with Clarence "Tom" Ashley during the 1920s, accompanying local square dances. In 1936 Smith was invited to perform at the White House, and during the 1940s he was recorded for the Library of Congress. During the 1950s and 1960s he met with acclaim through the folk revival and played at many festivals and concerts.

Smith's old-timey style is at the heart of many a modern banjo player's. He produced a wonderfully complex and invigorating sound from his banjo, and played the fiddle with great spirit and finesse, often bowing more than one string at a time. His lively vocals had a droll quality, coupled with a highly expressive voice. Clearly he thoroughly enjoyed his music, and he transmitted that pleasure to his audiences.

S·E·L·E·C·T·E·D R·E·C·O·R·D·I·N·G

America's Greatest Folk Instrumentalist
(FOLK-LEGACY FSA-17)

A delightful collection of songs and tunes, each revealing Smith's virtuosity. Essential for anyone even remotely interested in traditional old-time music. Among the highlights are the Child ballad "Devil and the Farmer's Wife" and two groups of banjo tunes.

Clarence "Tom" Ashley

Clarence Ashley, known as Tom from a childhood nickname, was one of the generation of musicians who straddled the fence between traditional and commercial music during the 1920s. Raised in the musical tradition of his family, he earned a living playing music professionally most of his life.

Ashley was born in 1895 in Tennessee and was brought up by his mother and his grandfather, whose last name he took as his own. His entire family was highly musical, and he participated in group sings and musical gatherings from an early age. When he was about 8 years old, his grandfather gave him his first banjo, and the boy's aunts set about teaching him how to play it. Ashley left school at the age of 10, and when he was about 12, he acquired his first guitar. He quickly mastered the instrument, and at 16, he was invited to join a traveling medicine show, an offer he accepted.

In 1914 Ashley married and set out to earn his living "busting," playing for tips on the streets. He teamed up with various musicians during this time but continued to play with the medicine shows during the summers; during the rest of the year he played with a succession of bands. The most famous of these, the Carolina Tar Heels, was formed in 1925.

The group, which made a number of recordings during the 1920s, had an unusual sound for a string band, because each of the members was highly skilled as a soloist, and the group employed the harmonica in a distinctive way.

The thirties and early forties saw Ashley continuing to earn his living through music. In 1943 he abandoned the medicine show circuit, however, and settled down to live on his farm.

Because of an injury to his finger, Ashley took a hiatus from playing the banjo until the 1960s, when he learned there was a new, urban audience for his music. He began to appear at concerts and festivals throughout the country, accompanied by Doc Watson, Gaither Carlton, Clint Howard, Fred Price, and others. They were the only traditional old-time band to establish itself on the urban scene, and Ashley continued to play until his death in 1967.

Ashley's approach to music was affected more by the musical traditions of his childhood than by the commercial influences of his professional career. His repertoire included ballads, hymns, fiddle tunes, old-time songs, and string band material, but both his singing and his banjo playing were firmly grounded in traditional styles. His banjo playing was distinctive and highly skilled, and his singing energetic but somewhat rough, partly the product of his advanced age. His superb recordings of the 1960s have been highly influential for over two decades.

S·E·L·E·C·T·E·D R·E·C·O·R·D·I·N·G·S

Old-Time Music at Clarence Ashley's
(FOLKWAYS FA 2355)
•
Old-Time Music at Clarence Ashley's, Volume 2
(FOLKWAYS FA 2359)

Two exceptional records of genuine old-time music, recorded in 1960–62. Ashley is joined by such high-caliber musicians as Doc Watson and Clint Howard. Volume 2, in particular contains some gems. Don't miss them.

Doc Watson

Doc Watson's music has been influenced by so many different strains that it defies classification. But one thing is certain: Watson is a musician of the highest caliber and has had tremendous impact on countless musicians playing in a wide variety of musical styles.

Blind from birth, Arthel "Doc" Watson was born in 1923 and grew up in northwest North Carolina, where he still lives. As a child he sang with his family and friends, and traditional ballads and old-time music played as large a part in his musical development as the commercial music on the radio.

The first instrument Watson learned to play was the harmonica, and he learned to fingerpick the guitar while he was a teenager. At the age of 17 he played at a fiddlers' convention in Boone, North Carolina, but his professional career didn't begin until he was 30, when he began playing a variety of music in a variety of bands, including the popular rockabilly style, which was a hybrid of rock and roll and country music. An audience for his traditional material developed during the

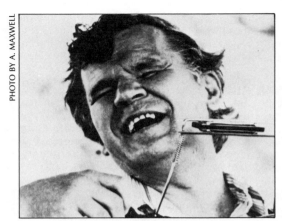

*Few musicians have bridged the gap
between traditional and popular music more
successfully than Doc Watson.*

early 1960s, however, and he joined with Clarence "Tom" Ashley to perform and to record a couple of albums.

Doc Watson's music is some of the most popular to come from the mountains. He has a warm, pleasing voice, but it is his seemingly effortless guitar playing that has made his reputation. An excellent fingerpicker, Watson has a flatpicking technique in a class by itself—remarkably fluid and clean, masterful without being flashy. He can easily hold his own with any of the fancier, bluegrass pickers, but his own style tends to be somewhat calmer, with the feeling of ease that accompanies the playing of a master, punctuated by stunning bursts of intricate lead work.

Although Watson is a traditional musician, his years of playing professionally have given him a smoothness unequalled by most other traditional musicians, and this has undoubtedly contributed to his enormous appeal—the integrity of his music coupled with a professionalism that makes it accessible to urban audiences.

S·E·L·E·C·T·E·D   R·E·C·O·R·D·I·N·G·S

The Doc Watson Family
(FOLKWAYS FTS 31021)

•

Doc Watson and Son
(VANGUARD VSD 79170)

•

Memories
(UNITED ARTISTS UA-LA 423-H2)

A giant like Doc Watson has many albums to his credit—this just a small sampling. *The Doc Watson Family* reveals just how deep Watson's traditional roots are. He is joined by family members in traditional ballads and hymns as well as instrumentals. *Doc Watson and Son* is an early collaboration between Watson and his son Merle, with whom he regularly performs (Merle is an accomplished multi-instrumentalist in his own right). It is an excellent collection of songs and tunes, sacred and secular, traditional and composed. *Memories,* the most commercial of the lot, shows his depth and breadth as he masters a wide range of material rooted in tradition, but with flashier arrangements than on the other albums.

The Commercial Connection

The fiddle and banjo had long been fixtures in traditional American music by the early years of this century, popular at dances and accompanying old-time songs. The guitar, however, had a revolutionary effect when it entered the mountains, for it added an essential rhythmic underpinning to the established banjo and fiddle music, and gave birth to the old-time string band.

The string bands incorporated a variety of influences. Although they generated much of their own material (some of it just plain silly), just as often they called upon the traditions that had nurtured them: fiddle tunes, ballads, old songs, and so on. The influence of black music was clearly discernible, sometimes in the guitar technique employed, sometimes in the material itself, which often was unmistakably of black origin. In one form or another, the early string bands were common sights in the early 20th century, at community gatherings and traveling medicine shows, among other places.

The 1920s, however, were a turning point in rural white music. The broadcasting and recording industries were getting off the ground, and although they had been directing their efforts primarily toward urban populations, a depression early in the decade threatened the entire entertainment industry. The record industry was particularly hard hit. In 1920, however, the Okeh Phonograph Corporation had experienced unprecedented success with black blues singer Mamie Smith's recording of "Crazy Blues." And Southern radio stations regularly invited local musicians to perform live over the air. The record companies began to realize that their salvation lay in specialized markets.

In 1923 Okeh's Ralph Peer, on a field trip to the South in search of new talent, recorded two songs by Fiddlin' John Carson, at the request of Okeh's Atlanta distributor. Peer thought Carson's singing dreadful, but pressed the records anyway because the distributor had promised to buy all the copies. To Peer's surprise, the records sold out almost immediately, and the distributor ordered more. Peer decided to pursue this newly discovered market in "hillbilly" artists.

Other talent scouts soon followed in Peer's footsteps, notably Frank Walker, who worked for Columbia and recorded a variety of groups, including Gid Tanner and the Skillet Lickers. Peer, for his part, brought a number of other groups to the fore, then decided to quit the music business for a while. Eventually he returned to the fold, however, this time for Victor, and once again headed into the field to search for talent. Late in July 1927, he arrived in Bristol, on the Tennessee-Virginia border, to hold auditions. He planted a news story about himself in the Sunday paper, and was immediately inundated with calls from people wanting to play for him. Through the auditions he held, he discovered the Carter Family, a now-legendary group of singers from the Virginia hills, and Jimmie Rodgers, who went on to become the first country music star to attract a national audience. Out of these beginnings grew today's phenomenally popular country music industry.

More than perhaps any other type of commercial music, however, the early country styles retained their connections with traditional music. Most of the early recording artists came from the hills, from backgrounds that fostered traditional music. The music industry may have just discovered the genre, but it had been a part of rural life for many years.

S·E·L·E·C·T·E·D R·E·C·O·R·D·I·N·G·S

Old-Time Ballads from the Southern Mountains
(COUNTY 522)
•
A Collection of Mountain Blues
(COUNTY 511)
•
Old-Time Fiddle Classics
(COUNTY 507)
•
Old-Time Mountain Guitar
(COUNTY 523)

Each of these albums represents one component of the early country music sound, from traditional ballads up through the influence of black blues, fiddle tunes, and black guitar styles. Many of the artists included in these anthologies played with the early string bands, yet their connections with more traditional kinds of music remain readily apparent on these recordings.

The Black Tradition

The black musical tradition in America has probably been more influential than any other in the development of popular music in the 20th century. Its fingerprints may be found on such well-established forms as jazz, rhythm and blues, soul and, quite directly, rock and roll. Yet the black tradition as such is not one tradition but many, and these frequently are hybrids.

The origins of black music in America generally are traced back to the music that the black slaves brought with them from Africa. Then, as today, rhythms, often complex, were an integral part of the tradition, and music figured prominently in the daily lives of the people. Slave traders found, in fact, that the high mortality rate among the captives bound for the New World was reduced if the blacks were made to dance regularly.

Once in America, the slaves were denied their customary outlets for music; they were forbidden to engage in their native traditions and ceremonies. But they found different ways of adapting the white man's music, which had been thrust upon them, into forms compatible with their own ravaged African culture. Generally these fell into work, religion, or entertainment-related activities.

Among the earliest identifiable forms of music that the slaves engaged in were field hollers—brief calls and cries that field workers used as a prime, albeit underground, means of communication. Also prominent were work songs and chants; these served to relieve the tedium of the work at hand, and also provided a rhythm by which a group task could be completed more quickly and efficiently. Structured much like sea shanteys, which served the same purpose, work songs usually had a lead singer, who set the pace, and his lines were answered by the rest of the group, in what has been called a call-and-response pattern.

The acculturation of the black in white America also required that he accept the white religion, and religious music came to be a highly significant component of the black musical tradition. Exposed to the sounds of their masters' hymns, the blacks would adapt the white Protestant music to fit the rhythms and inflections of Africa, creating in the process the spiritual, a sort of schizophrenic song praising God and decrying slavery.

Although music in West Africa was functional—there was no art music in the European sense—black slaves in America often were expected to provide entertainment as well as labor. Here again the African musical heritage played a formative role. From their homeland the blacks had imported the instrument that developed into the banjo. They also learned to play the instruments of their white masters, most notably the fiddle, but they approached them with an African aesthetic. Fiddle and banjo bands were common before the Civil War, and black and white musical forms continued to mingle in the development of such black ballads as "Staggerlee" and "Frankie and Albert" (later corrupted to "Frankie and Johnny"). How and when the guitar entered the black tradition remains a mystery, but the guitar was common in the Southwest, where the Mexican influence reigned supreme.

All these elements contributed to the development of what is the best-known and most popular black musical tradition: the blues. Reduced to its most basic, the blues is structured much like the call-and-response pattern of the old work songs, with the guitar or other accompanying instrument assuming the role of respondent. The classic formula is structured around 12 bars. The first line of the verse is sung—four bars—then followed up by an instrumental break. The line is then repeated, often with the addition of another word or phrase, and again the instrumental line. That is followed by the third and final line of the verse, which answers the first two lines and completes the rhyme.

Blues melodies are marked by the use of so-called blue notes, which are formed by flatting the third, fifth, and seventh notes of the scale, producing quarter tones. These notes fall between the notes of the standard Western scale, and while the human voice and such instruments as horns and stringed instruments can bend into them, fixed-pitch instruments like the piano construct the sound by creating dissonance.

The blues itself is an enormous and complex field best dealt with in books with the space to explore the subject in the depth it deserves. (See Peter Guralnick's *The Listener's Guide to the Blues*, for example). But through the folk revival, a number of black artists hailed as country blues singers came to the fore and were embraced by folk fans as the keepers of a living tradition. Many of these figures were not actually bluesmen per se—that is, they did not generate their own material so much as absorb songs from many sources, creating vast and varied repertoires. Often these musicians chafed at being called blues singers, and considered themselves "songsters" instead.

For many of these musicians, the acclaim the folk revival brought them was not the first they had experienced. During the 1920s, the recording industry had suddenly learned that black audiences were eager for records of their own music, and the record companies began scrambling to record black artists. With the coming of the Depression, however, the record industry had the wind knocked out of it, and the "race records," as the recordings of black artists were called, no longer were lucrative. Without records, many of the musicians retreated into obscurity until the revival of interest in blues and related forms in the middle of this century once again brought them into the public eye.

Leadbelly

Although his music demonstrated raw power rather than finesse, Huddie Ledbetter was the first black country musician to attain national prominence. Born in Louisiana in 1885, into a life of passion and blood, he grew up amid the spirituals, work songs, and hymns of his family and early on expressed interest in music. Before the age of 10 he had learned to play the accordion, but later his father gave him a guitar, and when he left home at the age of 16, it was the guitar he chose to take with him.

Leadbelly led a basically transient life, working at odd jobs and adding to his store of musical knowledge wherever he went. He became familiar with cowboy songs, as well as jazz and the blues. While in Dallas, he met up with legendary blues singer Blind Lemon Jefferson, and the two men traveled and played music together for a while.

Texas also brought Leadbelly trouble, however. In 1918 he was arraigned for assault and imprisoned for 6 years. From the other prisoners he continued to learn music, though, including hollers, chain gang chants, and work songs. In 1924 Leadbelly had the opportunity to perform for Texas governor Patrick Neff. Neff was so moved by his music that he released Leadbelly from prison in 1925.

FOLKLORE PRODUCTIONS INC.

Huddie Ledbetter (Leadbelly) sang his way out of prison and entertained largely white audiences in the early days of the revival.

Five years later Leadbelly was again imprisoned, this time in Louisiana. In 1933 John and Alan Lomax visited the prison farm where he was being held. Leadbelly eagerly cooperated with them, providing a wealth of music for them to record and, in turn, pleaded with them to intercede on his behalf with the authorities. The Lomaxes did, Leadbelly played for Louisiana governor O. K. Allen, and his sentence was commuted in 1934.

After his release, Leadbelly began a succession of concert appearances, arranged for him by the Lomaxes. He proved to be a dynamic performer and an excellent storyteller and appeared with the leading folk revivalists of the day, featured at such venues as the Village Vanguard and the Town Hall in New York. He traveled extensively, to the West Coast and to Europe. In 1936 the Lomaxes published a collection of his songs.

During a European tour in 1949, Leadbelly became seriously ill with the disease that was to claim his life. He returned to New York, and died of Lou Gehrig's disease on December 6 of the same year.

Leadbelly was a highly influential performer in both Britain and the United States; many musicians on both sides of the Atlantic continue to acknowledge a debt to him. Although he was conversant with a wide variety of instruments, he chose to concentrate on the 12-string guitar, and its full sound contributed immeasurably to his music. He had assimilated elements from myriad sources—his bass runs were closely akin to the boogie woogie beat, for example—and his guitar playing was widely imitated. He was not a fine singer in any conventional sense—his voice was nothing if not rough, and subtlety was nonexistent—but his music had a vitality that reflected his colorful life.

Leadbelly claimed to have written a number of important and, later, popular songs, among them "Good Night, Irene," "Rock Island Line," and "Midnight Special." And there has been much speculation about whether or not he actually did. Whatever the case, he was responsible for introducing them, and many others, to a wider audience.

S·E·L·E·C·T·E·D R·E·C·O·R·D·I·N·G

Leadbelly's Legacy, Volume 3
(FOLKWAYS FA 2024)

A ten-inch record, this album presents his material from 1935, the date of his first trip to New York. The fidelity is crude, but the sheer force of his music is everywhere apparent, in a selection of songs that concentrates on blues.

The Reverend Gary Davis

To put it bluntly, Gary Davis was possibly the greatest of the country blues ragtime guitarists.

Born in South Carolina in 1896, Davis grew up in a poor farming area. His first instrument was the banjo, which he taught himself to play, and at the age of 7, he made his first guitar out of a tin can. He also mastered the harmonica. During his teens he went to work as an itinerant musician, and in 1933 he was ordained as a minister. Sometime before then he was blinded.

During the 1930s he played with Blind Boy Fuller and Sonny Terry in North Carolina, and in 1935 he made his first recordings, which were basically religious. In 1940 Davis moved to New York and began playing on the streets and in the churches of Harlem. He quickly gained notice for his

FOLKLORE PRODUCTIONS INC.

The Reverend Gary Davis
was one of the most influential guitar
players of this century.

music and in time attracted not only record offers but a host of students as well. During the 1950s he recorded for Prestige and Stinson and appeared at coffeehouses. In 1959 he appeared at the Newport Folk Festival and, throughout the 1960s, at major festivals, even touring England. He had tremendous influence over other musicians, particularly younger white ones, and Peter, Paul, and Mary had a popular hit with his "Samson and Delilah."

Davis's health began to fail in 1971, and he died of a heart attack in 1972.

There were many singers better than Davis, but as a guitarist he was unsurpassed, and his impeccable, expressive ragtime style remains the ultimate standard for many. He once said that he played the guitar like the piano, an opinion that is borne out by his records, and reflects the influence of Blind Blake on his music. Although the overwhelming majority of his music was religious, for the younger audiences of the folk revival he began to resurrect more secular pieces, like "Candy Man" and "She Wouldn't Say Quit."

There was a consuming power to Davis's music, from his craggy, emotive singing to his virtuoso guitar playing, and the Reverend Gary Davis occupies a special and revered place in the annals of American music.

S·E·L·E·C·T·E·D R·E·C·O·R·D·I·N·G·S

The Reverend Gary Davis at Newport
(VANGUARD EVERYMAN SRV-73008)
•
Children of Zion
(KICKING MULE 101)

Two live albums, with an assortment of some of his best-known songs. The Newport album is a little rougher in terms of production, but the power of the music in no way is hampered. *Children of Zion* contains some of his best performances on record. Highly accessible and compelling music.

Mississippi John Hurt

There is perhaps no black blues singer better loved than Mississippi John Hurt. A native of the Delta area of Mississippi, Hurt was a professional musician for only a couple of very short periods in his life. He earned his living as a farm hand and made music for his own pleasure, a quality that no doubt contributed to his gentle, easygoing style.

Hurt was born in 1892 and began playing guitar at the age of 9. He had little exposure to the wandering musicians of the time and taught himself to play the instrument. He learned songs from the field hands and other workers in the area, and from the early part of the century on, he played at local dances and other events.

In 1917, two local white musicians were arranging to make a record for Okeh, and were asked about other musicians; they recommended Hurt. In 1928 Hurt recorded 8 sides, but only two were released. Later that year he recorded 5 more. Shortly after, the Depression hit, and Hurt vanished.

During the early years of the folk revival, a number of people tried to track Hurt down, but they were unsuccessful, and it was assumed he was dead. But blues collector Tom Hoskins, going on a clue on one of Hurt's records, "Avalon Blues," traveled to Avalon, Mississippi in 1963 and discovered Hurt alive and well. Hurt traveled with Hoskins to Washington, D.C., and his career was revived. He began playing professionally and the same year appeared at the Newport Folk Festival. He was the object of much acclaim and was given a new guitar at the festival's end. Articles appeared about Hurt in major journals, and he appeared at New York's Carnegie Hall, Town Hall, and on the "Tonight Show." Several albums of his music were released. Hurt's fame was short-lived, however, as he died in 1966, a mere 3 years after he was rediscovered.

Hurt's approach to music was unique among black musicians. He played the guitar primarily as an accompanying instrument, adhering to a fairly rigid picking pattern most of the time. His playing tended to be softer, more fluid, and less staccato than that of his contemporaries, and most of his repertoire wasn't blues at all. His singing was relaxed and pleasant but not showy. Perhaps the most memorable thing about his music was how much he enjoyed playing it.

S·E·L·E·C·T·E·D R·E·C·O·R·D·I·N·G·S

1928 Sessions
(YAZOO 1065)
•
The Best of Mississippi John Hurt
(VANGUARD VSD 19/20)

The first may lack the fidelity of the second, but it shows why blues aficionados were so interested in Hurt before his rediscovery. He was an excellent musican, capturing the emotional character that the blues were known for even though he steadfastly refused to consider himself a blues musician. *The Best of Mississippi John Hurt* was recorded live in 1965, a year before his death. His direct approach to his music was instantly engaging, and the years seemed to have robbed him of little of his technical ability.

Elizabeth Cotten

If the young Peggy Seeger hadn't wandered off in a Washington, D.C., department store one Christmas season during the 1940s, in all likelihood Elizabeth Cotten would never have received national attention for her music. For it was Cotten who found and returned the lost child, and as a result, the girl's mother, Ruth Crawford Seeger, hired Cotten to work in her home. Although Cotten had given up guitar playing many years earlier, at the behest of her church, she sometimes would play Peggy's guitar behind closed doors, and one day Peggy and her brother Mike overheard Cotten playing. The tune turned out to be "Freight Train," which Cotten had written when she was 12 years old. Libba Cotten's subsequent contribution to the folk scene is well documented. Since 1959 she has performed in numerous concerts and appeared at the leading national festivals.

Libba Cotten was born in 1893 and raised in Chapel Hill, North Carolina. One of her earliest wishes was for a guitar;

she would often play her brother's on the sly, and at the age of about 12, she went to work for 75¢ a month, doing housework to save money for her own instrument. She was entirely self-taught, down to her left-handed fingering on an instrument strung for a right-handed player. Cotten married at the age of 15, had one daughter, and joined the church, which prompted her to give up all secular music for 35 years.

Elizabeth Cotten's music is largely instrumental; she plays guitar and banjo instrumentals more than she sings, which may result from the fact that over the years she forgot the words to many of the songs but remembered the tunes. Her singing is somewhat weak, probably due to her advanced age more than anything else, but her guitar playing, reminiscent of John Hurt's, is a jaunty combination of blues, ragtime, religious music, and traditional song. She plays in both standard and open tunings and has a marvelous gift for learning music and arrangements.

S·E·L·E·C·T·E·D R·E·C·O·R·D·I·N·G·S

Folksongs and Instrumentals with Guitar
(FOLKWAYS FG 3526)
•
Shake Sugaree
(FOLKWAYS FTS 31003)

While the first record is considered by many to be the classic Libba Cotten LP, the second is of equal interest, as it contains original compositions. *Folksongs and Instrumentals* features several of her best-known tunes, however. One of the most striking things about both albums is what a good guitarist she is, even on the later LP, which was recorded when she was 73.

The Urban Revival: The Early Years

Songs with politically and socially relevant messages were nothing new in the 1930s and 1940s, when the so-called urban folk revival was getting under way. After all, the old broadsides that had filled the cities of Britain from the 16th century on frequently had attacked social ills. And the I.W.W. had been active in America during the second decade of this century, combining parodies of Salvation Army hymns with Communist doctrine. For that matter, the entire birth of the US was predicated on protest, and "Yankee Doodle" was proof that people had expressed themselves through song even in colonial times.

But at the height of the Depression, with scores of people destitute, there seemed to be more to say than ever before, and with record and radio to spread the word, the time had never seemed better to try and get it said.

Of course, the folk revival in the US didn't exactly begin in the 1930s. In some areas, notably Appalachia and other pockets around the country, traditional music had never been dead. Musicologist Charles Seeger and his first wife Constance (Pete's mother) learned that vividly when they traveled to Pinehurst, North Carolina, in the early 1920s in an attempt to introduce the hill dwellers to classical music. The locals listened politely, but the night the Seegers were ready to leave, they came forth with their own brand of music—and introduced the eminent scholar and his family to traditional American music.

In 1928 the Archive of Folk Song (now called the Archive of Folk Culture) was established at the Library of Congress as a repository for recordings and documents relating to traditional music. And Moses Asch, who founded Folkways Records in 1947, made his first recordings of folk music in the 1930s. John Lomax, and his son Alan, made thousands of field recordings for the Library of Congress during the 1930s and 1940s.

But the savage conditions that much of the country was living under seemed to call for something more. Many sought to use music as a rallying cry for social change. Aunt Molly Jackson, the union organizer and songwriter from Kentucky, had been using music as a call to arms for years; living in New York during the 1930s, she continued her struggle. Many people, newly informed and interested in the common man, sought to understand his culture and thus were drawn to traditional music.

Various political and musical activities brought together the leading figures of the early folk revival—Pete Seeger, Woody Guthrie, Leadbelly, Gordon Friesen and Sis Cunningham, Lee Hays, Josh White, and Will Geer, among others. Left-wing audiences were eager to hear the music of the people, and they were even more receptive when the music offered political messages compatible with their own views.

In 1940, Pete Seeger, Lee Hays, and Millard Lampell formed the Almanac Singers, a group who lived cooperatively and who were determined to use music to accomplish political and social goals. World War II and their earlier Communist affiliations ultimately destroyed them, but after the war their spirit continued in People's Songs, Inc., a loosely based organization that attempted to share songs and promote progressive causes through music. The organization went bankrupt after throwing its support behind Henry Wallace's unsuccessful campaign in 1949, but shortly afterward, Seeger and Hays formed the Weavers, along with Ronnie Gilbert and Fred Hellerman. All at once the record industry and the record-buying public took notice.

Woody Guthrie

On first listening, it might be hard to imagine why this diminutive, nasal-voiced man was one of the giants of American folk music, but Woody Guthrie was precisely that—a link between the rural traditions of his ancestors and the urban culture that came to dominate the 20th century.

Woodrow Wilson Guthrie was born on July 14th, 1912, in Okemah, Oklahoma. His childhood was marked by more than its share of tragedy—his sister Clara was accidentally burned to death; his father's business failed; and his mother, whose behavior increasingly was marked by erratic, unpredictable, and even violent outbursts, eventually was committed to a mental hospital. Yet his early years were also full of music. His mother, in particular, perpetuated the mountain ballads that had been part of her life in Tennessee, and Guthrie's paternal uncle was a fiddle player. As might be expected, young Woody took naturally to music. He took less naturally to schooling, however—he never completed high school—but was an avid reader and educated himself in a variety of subjects. At the age of 17 Guthrie left Oklahoma for Pampa, Texas, where he learned to play the guitar and formed his first musical group.

In 1933 Guthrie married Mary Jennings, the sister of one of the musicians in his band, but he quickly proved an unreliable husband and even worse as a father. In the mid-1930s, at the height of the Depression, he began to drift away from his home and his family, working odd jobs and riding the rails. He was already proving his mettle as a songwriter, and one source of inspiration was the I.W.W. *Little Red Songbook*.

Guthrie's travels took him to California, where he had family, and where he met Maxine "Lefty Lou" Crissman. He and "Lefty Lou" began playing music together, and they were able to find regular work on a Los Angeles radio station, quickly becoming an enormously popular act. When the Guthrie–Lefty Lou act began to grow stale, however, they decided to call it quits, and Guthrie proved less successful as a solo.

Late in the 1930s Guthrie began writing for the Communist *People's World* newspaper and playing for Communist Party functions as well as union meetings. Through these activities Guthrie met actor Will Geer, who had a special affinity for folk music. The two hit it off and often paired up to play for migrant workers and for left-wing causes.

When Geer left for New York to play in *Tobacco Road* on Broadway, he invited Guthrie to visit him there, and Guthrie took him up on the offer. In March 1940 Guthrie took part in a benefit Geer had organized for migrant workers. Also on the bill were Aunt Molly Jackson, Leadbelly, the young Pete Seeger, and others. But that event changed Guthrie's life, for at the concert he met Alan Lomax, and Lomax promptly took charge of Guthrie's career.

Lomax recorded Guthrie for the Library of Congress, and began to promote him, landing him spots on network radio. Offers began to pour in, Guthrie recorded some records and was swept into the limelight, with regular appearances on a number of shows. Eventually the old wanderlust hit him again, though, and he packed it in and headed for California.

THE COUNTRY MUSIC FOUNDATION LIBRARY AND MEDIA CENTER

*The legendary Woody Guthrie was
a transitional figure linking tradition
and revival in the 20th century.*

Meanwhile, his friends in New York were organizing into the Almanac Singers. After a limited success, they were asked to do a tour for the CIO during the summer of 1941, and they invited Guthrie to join them. He accepted but by the end of the tour, disputes and personality clashes had thinned their ranks, leaving only Guthrie and Seeger to carry on.

Returning to New York, Guthrie met Marjorie Mazia in early 1942 and promptly fell in love. His own marriage was on the skids, as was hers, and although their path was fraught with obstacles, they eventually married, in 1945. She remained an important, and stabilizing, influence throughout his life, and it was largely through her encouragement that Guthrie was able to complete his first book, *Bound For Glory,* published in 1943.

During World War II Guthrie served in the merchant marines, along with his close friend and sometime collaborator, Cisco Houston, and later in the army. After the war Guthrie became involved with People's Songs, Inc., and with the rise of the Weavers, who performed many of his songs, he was finally receiving recognition from the music business.

His own behavior was growing erratic, however, and he took to traveling again and drinking. In 1952 he was admitted to Brooklyn State Hospital, and his condition was eventually diagnosed as Huntington's chorea, the same hereditary disease that had claimed his mother's life. Fifteen years of deterioration followed, and on October 3, 1967, Guthrie died.

By today's standards, Guthrie's music may seem simplistic or even simpleminded. And admittedly, not everything he wrote was of the same high caliber as "This Land Is Your Land" or "Pastures of Plenty." He freely borrowed traditional melodies substituting his own, often topical words, and wrote nearly all his best-known material in this way. His extensive traveling gave him an unprecedented view of the country, and he wrote close to 1,000 songs about his experiences and attitudes; some songs, such as "Roll On Columbia," he even wrote on commission. Guthrie also wrote a large number of children's songs, a reflection of his lifelong love of rhymes and rhythms.

Guthrie's voice was somewhat rough, and his guitar playing rudimentary, influenced greatly by the Carter Family and, to a lesser extent, by black music. But he had tremendous personal charisma that spilled over into his music, and throughout his career he was known as a humorist as well as a musician. Musician, songwriter, author, poet, and philosopher, Guthrie continues to exert an enormous influence on American folk music over a decade and a half after his death. Truly he was one of the legends of our time.

S·E·L·E·C·T·E·D R·E·C·O·R·D·I·N·G·S

Bound for Glory
(FOLKWAYS FA 2481)
•
Dust Bowl Ballads
(FOLKWAYS FH 5212)

There's a certain amount of overlap between these records, but between them they cover many of Guthrie's best—and best-known—songs, although with an output as prodigious as his, it's virtually impossible for two records to include all of his most important material. *Bound For Glory*, which was edited by Guthrie's fellow ex-Almanac singer Millard Lampell, is particularly interesting, as it includes excerpts from his writings, delivered by his longtime friend, the late Will Geer. *Dust Bowl Ballads* is unified by its powerful subject matter; each of the songs relates in some way to the experiences of the Dust Bowl refugees of the 1930s. Both are invaluable as documents of one of the most important American singers and songwriters, and are quite accessible to any listener.

Pete Seeger

No other figure in American folk music has had the longtime visibility and involvement of Pete Seeger. A singer, songwriter, banjo player, and multi-instrumentalist, Seeger has had a lasting impact on so many aspects of the folk revival, it's difficult to calculate his influence.

Although he has spent the better part of his life fighting privilege, Seeger himself hails from an aristocratic, educated family. His father was the noted musicologist Charles Seeger; his mother Constance, a violinist. His childhood was marked by music—almost nonstop—both through his mother's love of classical music and his father's interest in traditional music. His first instrument was a ukelele, presented to him as a gift at the age of 8, but he didn't acquire his first five-string banjo until he was 17. He loved music passionately, but couldn't imagine making a living with it and set his sights on a career in journalism instead, a field that seemed particularly apt as Seeger became increasingly involved in politics.

The bitter economic realities of the 1930s came home to Seeger, however, when, after two years at Harvard, he left school to look for journalistic work. Although he was determined to find a job with a newspaper, he discovered that his aborted college education was not enough to convince New York employers to hire him. Increasingly, he turned to music, and in 1939 Alan Lomax invited him to work at the Archive of Folk Song, where he remained for the next year. During this period he made his first public appearance, at the same "Grapes of Wrath" benefit where Woody Guthrie met Alan Lomax, and Seeger, too, met Guthrie himself. Together they worked on a collection of political songs for Alan Lomax, and eventually they ended up traveling together as well. In 1940 Seeger, Lee Hays, and Millard Lampell organized the Almanac Singers. Before they could achieve any significant success, however, conservative blacklisting pulled them offstage, and the army diminished their ranks. There was a war on, and Seeger was drafted.

COURTESY OF THE RICHMOND ORGANIZATION

From the Almanac Singers to the **Clearwater,** *Pete Seeger has been actively involved in nearly every major development of the folk revial.*

After the armistice, Seeger, who had spent the war years working with USO entertainers on Saipan, began to put into effect a plan he had formulated while in the army. The result was People's Songs, Inc., the organization founded to further political aims through music. He threw his all into the project, publishing a newsletter and handling the group's finances. Their big break came when they were asked to provide the entertainers for Henry Wallace's progressive campaign. After Wallace's defeat, however, People's Songs, Inc., found itself bankrupt, and Seeger had no idea what he was going to do.

The answer came from music, of course. In the days after People's Songs folded, Seeger had been making music with

Ronnie Gilbert, Fred Hellerman and ex-Almanac Singer Lee Hays. They decided to form a group, and the Weavers were born, the first folk group to achieve commercial success. Their notoriety brought them political trouble, though, for their past left-wing activities made them fair game during the McCarthy era, and they were persecuted relentlessly. In 1955 Seeger and Hays were called before the House Un-American Activities Committee. Seeger refused to testify and was convicted of contempt of Congress and sentenced to a year in jail. He appealed the judgment, but the charge wasn't dropped until the early 1960s.

Even though Seeger had been one of the architects of the urban folk revival, by the time folk music hit the mainstream, powerful commercial interests were conspiring to shut him out. The most notable instance of this came when ABC-TV began airing a program called "Hootenanny" during the early 1960s. Because of his political activities, he was blacklisted from the program. Other musicians, many of them among the leading figures of the folk boom, responded by boycotting the show. Their support was heartening, but ultimately Seeger remained unable to perform on American television for 17 years.

Throughout his lengthy career, Pete Seeger's music has been shaped and motivated by his convictions. He has never shied away from controversy, and he has actively lived his beliefs. During the civil rights movement, he traveled to the South to lend his support to the blacks. During the Vietnam War, he was always available to speak—and sing—out. More recently, he was the mastermind behind the Clearwater project, which seeks to educate people about the environment and clean up the Hudson River.

Today Seeger would be something of a living legend—if he weren't so human. His music won't bowl anyone over with its complexity, but its accessibility is one of its most endearing traits. Seeger is a master at reaching his audiences, and it is through music that he communicates best, whether he's singing an old ballad or a topical song. He is an excellent banjo player and a wonderfully expressive singer, with a clear, warm tenor. An accomplished songwriter in his own right (he co-wrote "If I Had a Hammer" and "Wasn't That a Time" with Lee Hays), he was instrumental in exposing the songs of Bob Dylan and Malvina Reynolds to wider audiences.

Today, after more than 40 years as a folk musician, Pete Seeger remains an active, vital and, finally, much loved figure.

S·E·L·E·C·T·E·D R·E·C·O·R·D·I·N·G·S

Birds, Beasts, Bugs and Bigger Fishes
(FOLKWAYS FC 7611)
•
Broadside Ballads, Volume 2
(FOLKWAYS FH 5302)

Although two of Seeger's older records, these albums present two equally representative sides of Seeger's music. The first is sheer delight—lighthearted and fun, without the political messages of the second. *Broadside Ballads* is a collection of songs published by *Broadside* magazine, a periodical devoted to topical songs. Included are his versions of such classics as Malvina Reynolds's "Little Boxes," Bob Dylan's "Hard Rain's A-Gonna Fall," and Tom Paxton's "What did You Learn in School Today."

The Weavers

More than any other single group, the Weavers were responsible for launching the popular folk revival that began in the 1950s. Drawing on the traditional music of America, as well as countries from around the world, they developed their own stirring sound, and through the commercial market, they were able at last to reach the masses with folk music.

The original Weavers were Pete Seeger, Lee Hays, Fred Hellerman, and Ronnie Gilbert. They came together after the war to pursue the goals of People's Song, Inc., and after the demise of PSI, they continued to gather informally to make music. Their voices blended beautifully—Seeger's tenor, Hellerman's baritone, Hays's bass, and Gilbert's lush alto. Hellerman and Seeger were good instrumentalists as well.

The Weavers' first public appearance took place at the Village Vanguard in December 1949. Their first performances were less than successful, but the addition of management and the endorsement of poet Carl Sandburg attracted the attention of the press and, in time, the public. Eventually they were approached by a record producer from Decca, and in May 1950 they recorded "Tzena, Tzena," an Israeli song, and "Good Night Irene." In a matter of weeks, the record was a hit, and the Weavers were stars, playing the leading clubs in the country and making television appearances. The public simply couldn't get enough of their "new" music.

But also monitoring the Weavers' career was an FBI informant—and other right-wing interests flushed with the fever of McCarthyism. As the group became increasingly popular, they also became increasingly vulnerable. The onset of the Korean War was the final straw. The HUAC began calling artists and performers from all disciplines to testify. Slowly but surely, the Weavers were blacklisted. In February 1952 an FBI stool testified under oath that three members of the Weavers were members of the Communist Party. Almost overnight their careers plummeted. Even though their record sales were topping 4 million, no one would book them live. In spring 1953, they gave up the struggle.

Late in 1955, however, the Weavers reunited for a concert at Carnegie Hall. The concert was so successful, it prompted them to continue as a group once more. Seeger left in 1958, and was replaced by a succession of musicians: Erik Darling, Frank Hamilton, and Bernie Krause. The group disbanded in 1963.

The Weavers' music was one of the richest products of the urban revival. Their robust sound was possessed of remarkable variety and vitality, and it was perhaps inevitable that they would inspire numerous imitators. Yet the Weavers were unique, and they set the standard for the many groups that followed.

S·E·L·E·C·T·E·D R·E·C·O·R·D·I·N·G·S

The Weavers' Greatest Hits
(VANGUARD VSD 15/16)
•

The Weavers at Carnegie Hall
(VANGUARD VSD 6533)

Combining live and studio performances, the first album, a two-record set, encompasses virtually every song the Weavers made famous. *The Weavers at Carnegie Hall* is a now-classic album, documenting not only their triumphant reunion in 1955, but their enormous popularity and stirring music as well.

The Folk Scare

Singer-songwriter Bruce Phillips has coined the term "folk scare" to describe the surge of interest in folk music during the 1960s and the concomitant commercialization that accompanied its descent into the popular music market. And, Phillips's wry humor notwithstanding, the term is apt, for the musical products of the 1960s for the most part bore little resemblance to the traditions they claimed to represent. Ultimately they served to publicize rather than perpetuate traditional music, and while thousands of people were prompted to pick up guitars and, if they were perceptive, to explore the heritage that gave rise to the current craze, still more eagerly consumed the evidence of its corruption.

To be sure, a number of very fine musicians emerged at the time, people who not only understood traditional music but captured its spirit superbly. Dave van Ronk, Michael Cooney, and Tom Paxton are only 3 examples. And the New Lost City Ramblers, formed in 1958 and active throughout the following decade, were responsible not only for a resurgence of interest in string band music but for presenting many outstanding traditional musicians to the urban folk community.

It is a sad legacy of the era, though, that most people have come to associate folk music with the 1960s superstars: Joan Baez; Judy Collins; the Kingston Trio; Peter, Paul and Mary, and, perhaps, Odetta, Buffy St. Marie, and Phil Ochs.

The folk boom really started in 1958, when the Kingston Trio, following in the steps of the Weavers, had a hit song called "Tom Dooley." Never mind that the man from whom the song was collected, Frank Proffitt, a fine traditional singer and instrumentalist in his own right, never received a penny from the song's success. To a public hungry for more than the insipid pop music of the day, "Tom Dooley" and the Kingston Trio were *it*. Countless imitators sprang up immediately, some, like the Chad Mitchell Trio, better than others. In time ABC-TV even hopped on the bandwagon, with its "Hootenanny" show, a program that generated controversy by trying too hard to avoid it.

Things improved somewhat with the reintroduction of politics into the scene in the 1960s. Tom Paxton, still actively writing intelligent, clever songs today, and the late Phil Ochs contributed some excellent material, as did Bob Dylan, newly arrived in New York and steeped in the music of Woody Guthrie and in British folk music, some of which he lifted to create his own highly acclaimed songs. Some of the scene's leading figures, like Joan Baez and Judy Collins, made headlines for their political activities. Buffy St. Marie called national attention to the plight of the American Indian. In many people's minds, folk songs and protest songs became synonymous.

The beginning of the end came in 1965, at the Newport Folk Festival. To the dismay of the crowd, one of its heroes, Bob Dylan, came onstage playing an electric guitar. Despite the outrage of his fans, it signaled the beginning of something new, and slowly popularized folk music gave way to folk-rock.

Of course, there's no telling how many musicians, professional and amateur, would be missing from folk music today if the "folk scare" had never taken place. And urban audiences might have remained forever ignorant of the numerous traditional musicians who subsequently enriched their lives. Too often, however, it seemed that very little that resembled folk music actually made it onto vinyl and onto the airwaves, and anyone who could play three chords on a guitar was calling himself a folksinger.

Fortunately, the folk music revival didn't end when the commercial interests abandoned it in the late 1960s. Today there remains an active network of people around the country who play folk music both professionally and strictly for pleasure. Some familiar names from the 1950s and 1960s still make the rounds. Pete Seeger is still active, as are Dave van Ronk, Mike Seeger, and Tom Paxton. Others, no longer on the scene, like the New Lost City Ramblers and Malvina Reynolds, have left a legacy that perpetuates their influence. Many new musicians have emerged as well, spurred by the awareness of folk music they gained when it was America's pop music. Folk music is, after all, part of a process, and without big record companies orchestrating its development, its American manifestations now are richer and more varied than ever before.

The Continuing Tradition: Singing

Because today's musicians often are accomplished instrumentalists as well as singers, one cannot always make clear distinctions between the vocal and instrumental traditions. As has always been the case, folk music genres are tightly interwoven. In one breath Debby McClatchy may sing a Gold Rush song, for example, in the next an Irish ballad, then an original composition and finally proceed to play an old-timey instrumental. And such eclecticism is typical of many of the performers still active.

To some extent regional differences exist between different areas of the country. Gordon Bok's music is possessed of a New England character, and Bruce Phillips's of a Western one, but beyond mere subject matter, the distinctions are often hard to pin down.

Many people now play as much for their own enjoyment as for performances, but the professional folk musician is still with us. There is still a small circuit of clubs, although house concerts are increasingly popular and today's folk musicians generally remain outside mainstream music, in many cases deliberately so.

Gordon Bok

Bok has gained a considerable, and well-deserved, reputation as both a songwriter and interpreter of modern and traditional songs, and his music virtually embodies the spirit of his native Maine.

Although he is not a traditional singer in the conventional sense, Bok was raised with a singing tradition: his mother's family sang frequently, contemporary as well as folk music, and Bok himself began playing the guitar at the age of 9. His early exposure to a variety of musical forms has carried over into maturity and manifests itself in a broadminded approach to his repertoire. Gaelic, Mongolian, Eskimo, and South American songs and tunes have all found their way onto his recordings, and that eclecticism has been melded into a style all its own.

Bok is most closely associated with songs about the sea, however, which is, he says, one of the few things he knows anything about; for many years he worked on boats up and down the New England coast. But anyone familiar with his music would be quick to point out that music, too, is clearly among Bok's fields of expertise; he is a first-rate singer with a deep, rich voice, and an intricate yet understated guitar style that is as integral a part of his music as his voice and his characteristically nautical material.

He favors first-hand accounts—much of his material is, in fact, traditional—but, increasingly, he has turned to songwriting. Whenever he can't find a traditional song that says what he wants to say, he'll write one, although he insists that his primary purpose is not to be a songwriter.

Yet clearly Bok is a masterful songwriter. His original compositions are strikingly poetic, while remaining accessible, and he has an uncanny ability to focus on the human elements of a situation. One of the more unusual areas in which Bok has directed his energies are "cante-fables," or stories accompanied by music. Most prominent are those exploring seal legends. Using such traditional songs as "The Great Silkie" as his starting point, Bok has developed the mythology of the "seal people," who assume human form and interact with humans until some event prompts them to regain their animal form.

Some of Bok's most appealing work has been with Ed Trickett and Ann Mayo Muir. The trio, although loosely organized, has recorded several albums and sometimes performs together in concert. Their musical compatibility is evident in the material they choose—as with Bok's solo efforts, much of it is traditional and some of it is Bok's own, but enhanced through rich harmonies and additional instrumentation.

As memorable as his collaborative efforts are, though, ultimately it is Bok's singing, playing, and writing that linger in the listener's mind. And it's hardly any wonder. When music displays the fundamental integrity, both musically and philosophically, that Bok's does, it's hard not to notice.

S·E·L·E·C·T·E·D   R·E·C·O·R·D·I·N·G·S

Peter Kagan and the Wind
(FOLK-LEGACY FSI-44)

•

Bay of Fundy
(FOLK-LEGACY FSI-54)

•

With Ed Trickett and Ann Mayo Muir:
Turning Toward the Morning
(FOLK-LEGACY FSI-56)

Three of Bok's best albums. _Peter Kagan and the Wind_ includes not only a lovely selection of Bok's original songs and an impressive instrumental, but Bok's best-known cante-fable as well. With _Bay of Fundy_ Bok concentrates on songs, both his own and traditional, and most seem to share feelings of loneliness and desolation. _Turning Toward the Morning_ may be the most beautiful album ever recorded.

Ed Trickett

Ed Trickett is not a dazzling performer. You might call his music sincere and sensitive instead. But through understatement, he manages to capture the feeling of whatever song he sings, and ultimately delivers a powerful performance.

Trickett grew up in Washington, D.C., and was essentially raised by a musical grandmother and story-telling grandfather. As a child he studied piano and sang in the church choir; around the age of 11 he began playing an Arthur Godfrey ukelele. At a summer camp in New Mexico that he attended as a teenager, Trickett was introduced to the guitar, banjo, and dulcimer—and to Howie Mitchell. Through Mitchell Trickett met other members of the Chicago and East Coast folk scenes, people who played for their own pleasure and preserved the integrity of the music.

While in college Trickett regularly sought out people who shared his taste in music. During this time he met Ann Mayo Muir, and she in turn introduced him to Gordon Bok. The three began singing together, and the loosely organized trio remains a popular fixture in folk music.

One could probably not call Trickett a dynamic singer. He is known instead for seeking out unusual songs and singing them with great tastefulness and emotion. His guitar work tends to be quiet, although far more intricate than it appears on the surface. But he is an astonishing hammered dulcimer player with a complex style that has developed partly because he approaches the dulcimer as an accompanying instrument rather than as a lead instrument. His career as a psychology professor at the University of Maryland consumes much of his time, but he still manages to perform fairly regularly, both solo and with Bok and Muir.

S·E·L·E·C·T·E·D   R·E·C·O·R·D·I·N·G·S

The Telling Takes Me Home
(FOLK-LEGACY FSI-46)
•
Gently Down the Stream of Time
(FOLK-LEGACY FSI-64)

The Telling Takes Me Home is a lovely and subdued album with some of Trickett's best performances and some wonderful songs, including the title song and Bob Coltman's now classic "Before They Close the Minstrel Show." The second album is likewise enjoyable, but it lacks the cohesiveness of the first, despite its "unifying" theme of the cycle of life. Still, it is marked by some excellent material.

Guy Carawan
Singer, multi-instrumentalist, collector, festival organizer, and author—Guy Carawan is an enormously talented individual whose political and social convictions have been the source of much of his musical inspiration.

Carawan was born in California in 1927 and attended Occidental College and UCLA, where he received his master's degree in sociology. Because of a longtime interest in the South, he became involved in field work among Southern blacks and in Appalachia. He and his wife Candie were among the first whites to become active in the civil rights movement, and he was responsible for introducing the song "We Shall Overcome" to the movement. Since 1959 Carawan has been musical director of the Highlander Folk School in Tennessee.

Carawan's approach to music is eclectic but direct. Although he is an accomplished multi-instrumentalist, proficient on the guitar, banjo, whistle, Appalachian dulcimer, and especially the hammered dulcimer, for which he is well known, he accompanies his songs simply, never overpowering the material. His repertoire includes both traditional and contemporary music, but he presents it all with sensitivity and taste, and remains an enduring presence in American folk music.

S·E·L·E·C·T·E·D   R·E·C·O·R·D·I·N·G·S

Green Rocky Road
(JUNE APPAL 021)
•
Jubilee
(JUNE APPAL 029)

Both albums feature Carawan with an assortment of backup musicians. *Green Rocky Road* is stronger on instrumentals, especially Irish and American fiddle tunes, and *Jubilee* is weighted more toward songs. Carawan's rich, warm voice and outstanding instrumental capabilities make either one enjoyable listening.

Peggy Seeger

Like her brothers Mike and Pete, Peggy Seeger is a multi-instrumentalist whose immersion in traditional music during her formative years led her to become a highly accomplished musician in her own right. The child of Charles and Ruth Crawford Seeger, she began studying piano at an early age and learned to play the guitar at the age of 10. Frequent visitors to her parents' house when she was growing up exposed her to all kinds of traditional music, and in time she also picked up 5-string banjo, at which she excels; autoharp; dulcimer; and now English concertina.

Seeger attended Radcliffe and while in college began to perform in public. In 1955 she went to live in the Netherlands and subsequently traveled widely, even behind the Iron Curtain. In 1956, Alan Lomax asked her to come to England to take part in a television production, and as a result she met Ewan MacColl. She became part of MacColl's circle and was active in both the American and English folk scenes during the 1950s. She and MacColl became involved in a variety of projects together, married, and today reside in England.

Seeger appears on many of MacColl's records and has made many of her own. She tends to concentrate on American traditional music, especially that with a mountain flavor, but she is a highly skilled songwriter herself, known primarily for songs dealing with women's issues, a subject in which she is passionately interested. The best known of these is "I'm Gonna Be an Engineer," which confronts the issue of women's changing roles.

Seeger is a good singer, with a clear soprano, and she is an exceptional banjo player. She remains an important representative of America and American traditional music in Britain and Europe, returning regularly to the US for concert tours.

S·E·L·E·C·T·E·D R·E·C·O·R·D·I·N·G

Penelope Isn't Waiting Anymore
(ROUNDER 4011)

This collection of women's songs focuses on traditional material, mostly of American origin, but there are a few original Seeger compositions and a few English traditional songs as well. The material depicts women in a wide range of situations, often in roles of strength and decisiveness. An excellent introduction to Seeger and her combined traditional and contemporary aesthetic.

Michael Cooney

Michael Cooney performs so many different kinds of music and is so knowledgeable about his material that he often has been called a one-man folk festival. Indeed, an evening at one of his concerts exposes the audience to such a wide variety of musical styles, instruments, and anecdotes that they're so thoroughly entertained, they hardly notice that they've been educated as well.

Cooney grew up in Arizona, where, predictably, he was influenced by the folk boom of the 1960s. His first musical instrument was a ukelele, but eventually he graduated to a banjo and then a guitar. In high school he played in a folk trio, and even then he was drawn to the more unusual, lesser-known songs that today are his trademark. The appeal of folk music, he recalls, was that for the first time, here was a music that anyone could play and sing, without going through formal lessons and training (a perception that would be disputed, incidentally by many musicians).

Eventually Cooney came to California, and when someone finally offered him a significant amount of money to play folk music, he realized that he could make a living at it.

Cooney, who gathers his material from many different sources, plays everything from blues to English ballads, from American fiddle tunes to contemporary composed songs. He is highly proficient on both guitar and banjo (including 12-string guitar and fretless banjo), and he is a competent concertina player as well. His voice, while warm and distinctive, is not memorable for its perfect tone, but it is well suited to the simple arrangements and honest approach he takes to his music. He shies away, in fact, from anything smacking of commercialism and makes a concerted effort to avoid slickness, a policy that sometimes makes his music sound a little rough around the edges.

A former columnist for *Sing Out!* magazine, Cooney was seriously injured in an automobile accident in 1979. Since recovering, however, he has resumed his musical career, continuing to sing the songs that no one else bothers to learn.

S·E·L·E·C·T·E·D   R·E·C·O·R·D·I·N·G·S

Singer of Old Songs
(FRONT HALL FHR-07)
•
Still Cooney After All These Years
(FRONT HALL FHR-016)

Cooney's singularly eclectic repertoire is well represented here, with everything from old blues to fiddle tunes to British ballads and everything in between. The albums are pleasant, and Cooney is obviously an excellent musician, but he is best seen live.

Debby McClatchy

This diminutive woman with the big voice is a consummate musician whose taste—and expertise—run to traditional ballads and tunes, early country songs, original compositions, and even vaudeville. A native of San Francisco, her childhood was divided between the city and the gold-rush country of the Sierra Nevada, and her schizophrenic background is undoubtedly what gave rise to her fascination with the songs and lore of the Gold Rush, and perhaps to her eclecticism as well.

McClatchy is a wonderful singer, with a radiant alto voice that she employs in an expressive but subtle manner. She is as comfortable playing an old-time fiddle tune on the banjo as she is singing, and the banjo, dulcimer, guitar, and concertina are her particular areas of instrumental expertise. The Gold Rush material is probably the most distinctive part of her repertoire, but she is equally adept at traditional ballads and especially favors those from Ireland. She tends to write songs to fill gaps in her repertoire and for personal expression.

Debby McClatchy has lived in many different places and played with many different musicians, all the time developing and polishing her craft. In 1976 she recorded an album with the Red Clay Ramblers, with whom she played in the show *Diamond Studs* for 3 months.

S·E·L·E·C·T·E·D R·E·C·O·R·D·I·N·G·S

Lady Luck
(GREEN LINNET SIF 1017)
•
Off to California
(WILDEBEEST WB 006)
•
With the Red Clay Ramblers:
Debby McClatchy with the Red Clay Ramblers
(GREEN LINNET SIF 1003)

Each of these albums represents well the breadth and excellence of McClatchy's repertoire, but *Off to California* is the jewel of the lot, with the wonderful "Banks of the Sacramento" and an excellent version of Robin and Linda Williams's "Murderers on the Cumberland Plateau" especially worthy of note. *Lady Luck* also features some outstanding material, as does the album with the Red Clay Ramblers, who provide impeccable and imaginative accompaniment to McClatchy's vocals.

Rosalie Sorrels

Rosalie Sorrels plays many roles—singer, songwriter, storyteller, folk song collector, and mother. And although she is something of a fixture on the folk scene, by no means is her repertoire dominated by folk music.

Sorrels was born in Idaho, into a family with a musical tradition of its own, from her father's opera singing in the shower, to her mother's 1930s and 1940s pop jazz tunes, to her grandmother's Anglo-American singing tradition. Marriage brought her to Utah, where she took a class in American folk music and became interested in collecting and singing, and she gained a reputation in the area for her music. Around 1967, after her marriage broke up, she turned professional, in an attempt to support her brood of five. She has spent much time on the road, and the ubiquitous Sorrels turns up at festivals and concerts all over the U.S.

Sorrels places her individual musical stamp on every song she touches. She often adopts a lusty approach to her music, singing in a rich, sultry voice and crooning rather than belting out a song. She is an adventurous, gutsy woman, committed to women's issues, and her own songs often confront difficulties she has encountered in her own life.

The problem with having a personal style as strong as Sorrels's is that too often the music all sounds the same. And sometimes Sorrels's music cries out for more variety, both in approach and in repertoire. The problem is augmented by the fact that her guitar playing is rudimentary and does little to add interest.

Still, Sorrels is a good, if occasionally static, singer, and her engaging personality can often carry the music when the songs themselves grow a trifle monotonous.

S·E·L·E·C·T·E·D R·E·C·O·R·D·I·N·G·S

If I Could Be the Rain
(FOLK-LEGACY FSI-31)
·
Always a Lady
(PHILO 1029)
·
The Lonesome Roving Wolves
(GREEN LINNET SIF 1024)

If I Could Be the Rain is a collection of original songs and songs by Sorrels's longtime friend Bruce Phillips; *Always a Lady* features songs largely by contemporary songwriters, and is more produced. Both albums are marked by Sorrels's unique vocal style. *The Lonesome Roving Wolves* is the least typical of her albums, but it is also the best, with a splendid group of traditional songs from the West, sung unaccompanied or with minimum accompaniment. It would be wonderful to hear Sorrels do more material like this, as she's exceptionally good at it.

The Continuing Tradition: Black

It is a sad fact that the black blues and songster traditions today are being carried on largely by white people. With a few notable exceptions, like Taj Mahal, who also plays rock and soul, and Sparky Rucker, the people who play country blues and ragtime guitar today came to the genre through the folk revival. Though some mastered the styles, they did not grow up with the traditions.

Of course, it's largely due to their efforts that these musical traditions will be preserved and passed on to other musicians through more than scratchy records from the 1920s or recordings of old men from the 1960s. And chances are, the ranks of country blues and ragtime aficionados would be considerably thinner without them.

Labels often are more limiting than accurate, and among the current crop of country blues players, that is truer than ever before, as most regularly explore many different kinds of music. Stefan Grossman, for example, the Reverend Gary Davis's best-known disciple, composes contemporary music in addition to playing blues and ragtime guitar. Dave van Ronk applies his unique vocal and guitar styles to Joni Mitchell songs as well as those from the black tradition. John Fahey and Leo

Kottke have used the blues mainly as a point of departure for their own distinctive musical styles.

Whatever their orientation, though, acoustic guitarists throughout the world today continue to be strongly influenced by black musical traditions.

Dave Van Ronk

This whiskey-voiced singer-guitarist has been a fixture on the folk scene since the 1960s, when he and numerous other talented musicians congregated in New York's Greenwich Village. But while many of the others passed from public notice and now are largely forgotten, Van Ronk has remained a popular and respected figure.

Dave van Ronk grew up in New York and originally was drawn to jazz. He knew little of the blues until he chanced upon Furry Lewis's version of "Stackolee." Once introduced to the genre, he was hooked. Because he had no other prototype to follow, he developed his singing style by listening to old blues recordings. As he became increasingly proficient, he began appearing regularly in clubs around New

COURTESY OF FOLKLORE PRODUCTIONS, INC.

His raspy voice and vibrant finger-style guitar playing have ensured Dave Van Ronk's continuing position of prominence in the American folk scene.

York, gaining a following. By the mid-sixties Van Ronk established himself as one of the few musicians, black or white, to capture white middle-class audiences by playing blues.

Van Ronk has cited the Reverend Gary Davis, Mississippi John Hurt, and Josh White as some of his primary influences. Although his style and repertoire are dominated by the blues, his taste actually is highly eclectic, touching on contemporary songwriters, piano rags, swing tunes, and even original compositions. His expressive, rasping singing is a perfect foil to his driving, dynamic guitar work; his playing is bright, clean, and gutsy while his singing is hoarse and aggressive, a style compatible with that of the tradition on which he draws, yet not imitative.

An extraordinary musician and performer, Dave Van Ronk continues to be popular and influential.

S·E·L·E·C·T·E·D R·E·C·O·R·D·I·N·G·S

Black Mountain Blues
(FOLKWAYS FTS 31020)
•
Dave Van Ronk, Folksinger
(PRESTIGE 7527)
•
Sunday Street
(PHILO 1036)

The Folkways release, one of Van Ronk's first albums, contains a liberal dose of the blues for which he became known, although there is a curiously calypso version of "Careless Love" as well. *Dave Van Ronk, Folksinger* is a little more eclectic and subdued, but a first-rate record as well. Notable are his version of "Cocaine Blues" and a sensitive rendition of "Hang Me, Oh Hang Me." *Sunday Street* is more varied, although only a little, with excellent versions of Joni Mitchell's "That Song About the Midway" and the classic "Would You Like to Swing on a Star?"

Stefan Grossman

When it comes to the guitar, few people have had the impact or visibility of Stefan Grossman. For Grossman not only is a distinguished instrumentalist, he is the author of numerous instruction books and, as the founder of Kicking Mule Records—which concentrates on recording acoustic instrumentalists, especially guitarists—he has been responsible for recording and producing many fine instructional records as well.

Born in Brooklyn, New York, in 1945, Grossman was drawn to folk music while in high school and used to visit Greenwich Village to listen to the musicians who played there. This was the heyday of the folk revival, and the young Grossman eventually encountered the Reverend Gary Davis and began studying guitar under his tutelage. Grossman became Davis's star pupil, and studied with him for two years. He went on to learn from other prominent ragtime and country blues guitarists as well, such as Mississippi John Hurt, Son House, Skip James, Mance Lipscomb, and Fred McDowell. During the 1960s he played in several bands, including the Even Dozen Jug Band, which he formed, and the Fugs, and late in the decade he went to Britain, where he now lives.

Grossman's guitar playing clearly is indebted to the bluesmen from whom he learned, with crisp, percussive styling, but he has recorded countless original numbers as well. Most recently, he has been working with John Renbourn in an unusual collaboration that juxtaposes Renbourn's classically influenced medieval and Renaissance style with his own blues orientation. The marriage has been a success, however, with innovative and highly listenable music as the product. As a singer, Grossman leaves a lot to be desired, but his barbed humor and witty repartee make him a lively performer.

S·E·L·E·C·T·E·D R·E·C·O·R·D·I·N·G·S

How to Play Ragtime Guitar
(KICKING MULE KM 115)
•

With John Renbourn:
Stefan Grossman and John Renbourn
(KICKING MULE KM 152)

How to Play Ragtime Guitar is, as the title indicates, one of Grossman's instructional records, but it is enjoyable, if somewhat sterile, as many Kicking Mule records tend to be. Technically, it is most impressive, however, and the fundamental life of the material manages to break through. Grossman's collaboration with Renbourn may be the finest thing he's ever done, and this album, their first together, is a superb work. All material is original, except the reworking of a Charlie Mingus number, and the teaming-up of two such different but obviously compatible talents has resulted in refreshing and progressive music.

The Continuing Tradition: Old-Timey

It is largely through the efforts of the New Lost City Ramblers in the 1960s and 1970s that string band and old-time mountain music is as popular today as it is. In fact, old-timey music, as it has come to be called, may well be the most popular segment of the folk revival. Over the years there have been many professional old-timey bands, the most notable, of course, the group that began the revival. Most such groups stick pretty much to the tunes and songs of the mountains and the old string bands, but some, like the superb Red Clay Ramblers, use old-timey music as the basis of their own unusual style. There are also solo artists actively pursuing old-timey music, and numerous well-known musicians in both pop and folk fields at one time played string band music.

The liveliest segment of the old-timey tradition, however, is probably that comprised of people who play informally, at parties, dances, and the like. Everywhere folk musicians gather, large groups invariably congregate to play "Sail Away, Ladies," "Shady Grove" and other classics of the string band and country dance band repertoire.,

Sometimes, in large doses, old-timey music can get tiresome, but it remains a popular and vital link with America's musical past.

New Lost City Ramblers

At a time when the public was embracing the more commercial manifestations of "folk music," a trio of musicians from the East coast were delving back into the rural origins of traditional American music. The New Lost City Ramblers, as they called themselves, came together in 1958, bound by their common love for authentic string band music and their desire to stay as close to their sources as possible—at times even

The New Lost City Ramblers, shown here in their original configuration of Mike Seeger, Tom Paley, and John Cohen (clockwise from right), launched a revival of interest in early string band music.

reproducing the mistakes captured on the early recordings. But although they drew directly from the old string band recordings, their sound was their own, and they evoked the feeling of the earlier music rather than copying it.

The original members of the group, Mike Seeger, Tom Paley, and John Cohen, were all multi-instrumentalists, and the group quickly became known for crowding the stage with instruments and for interminable interludes of tuning during their live performances. At the time, playing traditional music in a traditional way was highly innovative, and the band proved enormously influential. As a result of the Ramblers' efforts to present the music to a wider audience, they presented many traditional musicians to the urban audiences.

In 1962, however, Tom Paley left and was replaced by Tracy Schwarz, an exceptionally good fiddler with a stronger country orientation than the others. Schwarz's inclusion prompted the group to pursue bluegrass and later country music and even Cajun music, an interest shared by Seeger and Schwarz. And late in the decade, the Ramblers became involved in some of the political activities that dominated the 1960s.

The New Lost City Ramblers are now defunct as a group, having disbanded officially in 1979, but the individual members continue to perform on their own and remain respected figures.

S·E·L·E·C·T·E·D R·E·C·O·R·D·I·N·G·S

The New Lost City Ramblers
(FOLKWAYS FA 2396)
·
Songs from the Depression
(FOLKWAYS FH 5264)
·
Remembrance of Things to Come
(FOLKWAYS FTS 31035)

The New Lost City Ramblers and *Songs from the Depression* feature the first configuration of the band, with Tom Paley. The first includes a fine selection of old-timey songs and tunes, with an emphasis on string band music. Like any body of work born out of hard times, *Songs from the Depression* has a unity and strength not often matched and is an excellent album. *Remembrance of Things to Come,* with Tracy Schwarz taking Paley's place, reflects the stronger bluegrass orientation that later became the group's hallmark.

Red Clay Ramblers

The Red Clay Ramblers aren't a string band, exactly. But then they aren't a bluegrass, jazz, gospel, or swing band, either. In fact, they simply cannot be pigeonholed, and that, along with their highly polished arrangements and their sense of fun, are their primary strengths.

As their name indicates, the band hails from North Carolina, and although they started out as a string band when banjo player Tommy Thompson, mandolinist Jim Watson, and fiddler Bill Hicks formed the group in 1972, early on they branched out into variants and even musical styles that were altogether unrelated. They recorded their first album on Folkways; pianist Mike Craver joined the group in 1973. After the release of their second album, *Stolen Love,* trumpet and bass player Jack Herrick joined, and that lineup existed until fairly recently, when Clay Buckner replaced the departing Bill Hicks. In the mid-1970s, they even performed in an off-Broadway musical, *Diamond Studs: The Life of Jesse James.*

The Red Clay Ramblers' departure from standard string band fare is immediately apparent in their unorthodox instrumentation, and it extends to their choice of material, which is eclectic, frequently lighthearted, and often tongue-in-cheek. And it certainly is shaped by their musical abilities, which are formidable, to say the least. They draw their material from a variety of sources, some of which are members of the band themselves. Mike Craver and Tommy Thompson in particular are excellent songwriters, and produce material that is unique and often enigmatic. They also continue to play the string band music that brought them together, as well as early jazz, Irish traditional tunes, gospel, Stephen Foster songs—virtually any genre of music that appeals to them. Their arrangements are highly inventive, marked by unsurpassed harmonies and their unique instrumental lineup. To whatever they play, they bring conviction, expertise, and rollicking good humor.

S·E·L·E·C·T·E·D R·E·C·O·R·D·I·N·G·S

Merchants Lunch
(FLYING FISH FF 055)
•
Chuckin' the Frizz
(FLYING FISH FF 089)
•
Hard Times
(FLYING FISH FF 246)

You can't go wrong with any of the Red Clay Ramblers' records, especially the later ones. *Merchants Lunch* has to be one of the best albums ever recorded by anyone. And superlatives, you'll find, are not out of place. *Chuckin' the Frizz* is also good, although not as memorable as its predecessor; the same can be said of *Hard Times*. Try them; you'll like them.

Mike Seeger

It was perhaps inevitable that someone with Mike Seeger's background would end up a musician. Born in 1933 into the prominent Seeger family, he grew up hearing field recordings of traditional musicians, and by the age of 12 had begun playing the autoharp. Around the age of 18 he began pursuing music in earnest, and learned guitar, banjo, mandolin, fiddle, harmonica, dobro, and dulcimer, becoming a musician with varied, versatile, and far-reaching talents.

When Seeger first started playing music actively, he dished up the standard urban revival fare, although with a somewhat more traditional orientation. Eventually he and his younger sister Peggy began playing together around Washington, D.C., and for square dances. During the mid-fifties, he met Hazel Dickens and Bob Baker, whose influence prompted him to begin playing bluegrass. In 1958 he formed the New Lost City Ramblers with John Cohen and Tom Paley, and also won the first prize for banjo in the Galax Old Time Fiddlers' Convention in Virginia.

Although the New Lost City Ramblers occupied much of his time and attention over the next few years, he was active making field recordings for Moe Asch of Folkways Records, an activity that doubtless aided him in his mission to bring traditional musicians to the attention of urban audiences. In the late 1960s he began performing more; both on his own, and with the Strange Creek Singers, a group formed with Hazel Dickens, Alice Gerrard, Tracy Schwarz, and Lamar Grier.

Seeger has recorded myriad albums, both solo and with Alice Gerrard, his sister Peggy, the Ramblers, and the Strange Creek Singers, and he has performed throughout the world. He has also served as an advisor to numerous organizations devoted to traditional music.

S·E·L·E·C·T·E·D R·E·C·O·R·D·I·N·G

Old Time Country Music
(FOLKWAYS FA 2325)

Recorded fairly early in his career, this lively album was released after the formation of the New Lost City

Ramblers, and like that group's early configuration, concentrates on old-time string band music and ballads. Seeger clearly is an inventive and accomplished musician, and overdubbing has enabled him to play virtually all the instruments in the robust arrangements that characterize the record.

John McCutcheon

The hammered dulcimer is his trademark, but John McCutcheon is actually highly proficient on a wide variety of instruments. A native of Wisconsin, McCutcheon came to the South in the early 1970s, and has since been active in an array of musical activities, including collecting, calling square dances, teaching, organizing festivals, and, of course, playing and performing music.

Widely acclaimed as one of the finest hammered dulcimer players in the world, McCutcheon has performed throughout the U.S., playing for Harlan County picket lines as well as concerts, workshops, festivals, and informal gatherings. His material reflects his love for Appalachian music in all its forms, ranging from Sacred Harp hymns to bouyant hoe-downs, from traditional Child ballads to the songs of modern writers like Si Kahn. Like Mike Seeger, McCutcheon is deeply committed to promoting traditional musicians, and through his own concerts and festivals, has brought many into the public eye.

McCutcheon's own music is perhaps best characterized by its unending vitality and perceptiveness. He is immersed in traditional music, and possesses the sensibilities of the genre. His multi-instrumental approach, which includes fiddle, banjo, guitar, autoharp, dulcimer, harmonica, and Jews harp as well as hammered dulcimer, affords him unsurpassed versatility, and he is a fine singer as well.

S·E·L·E·C·T·E·D R·E·C·O·R·D·I·N·G·S

How Can I Keep From Singing?
(JUNE APPAL 003)
•
The Wind that Shakes the Barley
(JUNE APPAL 014)
•
Barefoot Boy with Boots On
(FRONT HALL FHR-021)

Just as McCutcheon is possessed of a wealth of musical talents and interests, so he is prolific in terms of recordings. The first, McCutcheon's debut album, is a collection of tunes and songs. *The Wind that Shakes the Barley* focuses exclusively on the hammered dulcimer; it is an eclectic selection of material, from Bach to ragtime and everything in between. *Barefoot Boy* has more songs, and he is joined by fellow dulcimer player Paul van Arsdale.

Songwriters

Despite the popular wisdom that holds that folk music is anonymous, in the US there is a long history of composed music. The tendency has been, however, for folk musicians, old and modern, to write their own material when nothing traditional or already written exists to fill a need. Aunt Molly Jackson and her half-sister Sarah Ogan Gunning, for example, penned songs to express their outrage at the mine operators during the 1920s and 1930s. Woody Guthrie likewise adapted old material and created new to expose the plight of the Dust Bowl refugees during the 1930s. The pattern has continued up to the present, sometimes with political overtones, sometimes without. During the 1960s, of course, there were so many good folk-oriented songwriters—among them Bob Dylan, Eric Andersen, Tom Paxton, and Phil Ochs—that *folk song* began to lose its meaning, applied indiscriminately to anything with guitar accompaniment.

As folk gave way to folk-rock and then MOR apathy, however, the ranks of folk-oriented songwriters thinned, or at least shifted. Without an audience for the politically oriented material, Phil Ochs, unable to produce songs for a new, apathetic America, committed suicide. Much of Malvina Reynolds's music, on the other hand, has remained well-loved but less frequently played. Of the 1960s songwriters, Tom Paxton alone is continuing successfully the blend of personal and topical songs that originally thrust his name into the limelight. And his name has been joined by that of Bruce Phillips, a songwriter of considerable talent and feeling, and others, like Holly Near, who write with more passion than humor. Still other songwriters, like Gordon Bok and Bill Staines, are creating original music that emulates traditional song, while Mary McCaslin and Jim Ringer and Robin and Linda Williams are incorporating a variety of influences in their country-flavored work.

The folk scene has been the incubator for some of the finest songwriting in the country. And, as much as any other component, songwriting is a vital part of the continuing folk tradition.

Tom Paxton

Of all the songwriters who proliferated during the 1960s, none has retained ties to the folk audience as consistently as Tom Paxton. A writer of consummate taste, sensitivity, and skill, Paxton not only produced such well-known chestnuts as "Ramblin' Boy," "The Last Thing on My Mind" and "I Can't Help But Wonder Where I'm Bound," which remain among the best-loved and best-known songs of the revival, but over the years he has continued to write intelligent, singable songs.

Paxton, who grew up in Oklahoma, originally attended the University of Oklahoma, intending to pursue a career in theater. Upon discovering folk music, however, his aims shifted, and in 1960 Paxton arrived in New York and became part of the Greenwich Village folk scene, playing in clubs and coffeehouses. Although his early repertoire was an amalgamation of traditional and modern folk song, he soon began writing his own songs, and by 1966 or 1967 he was performing his own material exclusively. Because many of his songs were topical, they were quickly included in such magazines as _Sing Out!_ and _Broadside,_ which gave them wide exposure.

Few songwriters in any genre can match Paxton's skill. While he never shies away from controversial subjects (some of his more recent songs confront Anita Bryant's crusade against gays, the Abscam fiasco, and Congress' bailout of Chrysler), such songs comprise perhaps a quarter of his repertoire, and the rest is given over to songs about love, interpersonal relations, and virtually any subject he feels he can write about. "Technically I'm not a folk singer," he has said. "I don't sing folk songs; I sing my own songs. And they're songs which owe an enormous debt to traditional music-making styles, traditional song.... If I hadn't been a lover of folk music, I wouldn't be writing the way I write."

S·E·L·E·C·T·E·D R·E·C·O·R·D·I·N·G·S

The Compleat Tom Paxton
(ELEKTRA 7E-2003)
•
Heroes
(VANGUARD VSD 79411)
•
The Paxton Report
(MOUNTAIN RAILROAD 52796)

Unfortunately, most of Paxton's recorded efforts don't live up to the promise of his concerts. While the songs certainly are strong enough to stand on their own, his stage manner is so totally disarming and his presentation so simple and straightforward, the rather produced efforts on record seem only shadows of the live performances. _The Compleat Tom Paxton,_ the artist's last recording for Elektra, is a live double album and captures a little of his magic, although with the sometimes intrusive backup of a band. _Heroes_ includes some of his best later songs, and _The Paxton Report_ continues in the same vein, with some of his best material since the 1960s.

U. Utah Phillips

Bruce "U. Utah" Phillips, the Golden Voice of the Great Southwest, may be, as he puts it, a rumor in his own time, but his songs are real enough. Fiercely committed to exposing and righting the plight of the underdog, he is a songwriter of piercing sensitivity. And as a performer he makes his message more palatable, if no less potent, with large doses of outrageous humor, puns, and stories.

Phillips was born in Cleveland in 1939 but moved with his family to Utah in 1947. His parents were union organizers who took pains to see that his education included the proletarian view of history and society. It was his experiences in Korea, however, that he says made a radical of him, for he saw how the Korean culture was being eroded by the presence of the foreign army.

When Phillips returned to the US, he rejoined the I.W.W., an organization to which he had belonged many years before, and threw himself into community activities that spoke to his convictions. He also began writing songs, adapting I.W.W. material from the *Little Red Songbook*. He became active in myriad political causes, joined the Peace and Freedom Party and ran as its Senate candidate in 1968. He decided the political route was not for him, however, and, in finding himself unemployable in Utah, left the state and began to pursue a musical career. In 1969 he began traveling and singing in earnest, and in 1974 he settled in Spokane, Washington.

Phillips is passionately concerned about anyone stuck in a situation that robs him or her of dignity and sense of worth. He has ridden the rails with the hoboes, written many songs about them, and been invited to their annual convention. Yet his songs deal with numerous other subjects, too. He loves railroading and the American West and has written extensively about them as well. One of his best songs, "Touch Me" is a love song.

Bruce Phillips is a highly visible member of the folk scene, a fixture at festivals, and an outspoken but warm performer well loved by his audiences. He is an expert storyteller and a competent but undistinguished musician, but a marvelous performer, whose humor counterbalances the poignancy of his songs. A genuine character, he is in a direct line of descent from such other concerned songwriters as Aunt Molly Jackson and Woody Guthrie. Don't miss him—he's one of a kind.

S·E·L·E·C·T·E·D R·E·C·O·R·D·I·N·G·S

Good Though!
(PHILO 1004)

All Used Up: A Scrapbook
(PHILO 1050)

The title *Good Though!* is pulled from the outrageous story Phillips has astutely included on the album, as storytelling is one of his greatest strengths. But the record, which centers around a railroading theme, is full of excellent songs, most original. Replete with sound effects and narration in between cuts, it is a wonderful collection, and "Moose Turd Pie" alone is worth the price of admission. *All Used Up* contains a selection of topical songs, many original, and several from such sources as the I.W.W. and Woody Guthrie. It includes some of Phillips's best performances on record.

Bill Staines

If sometime a simple, melodic song catches your fancy, and later you find it running relentlessly through your head, there's a good possibility that song was written by Bill Staines. Since the late 1970s, Staines's reputation as a songwriter has been growing rapidly, as increasing numbers of his peers record his songs on their own albums, and his music is so accessible, it has been insinuating itself into many people's ears.

Yet because Staines's music is often low-key, it is sometimes difficult to pinpoint exactly why it is so compelling. The answer undoubtedly lies in its simplicity. His songs usually are very easy to sing, highly melodic, and deal with universal themes in a straightforward manner. His lyrics seldom dazzle, and his guitar accompaniments, while tasteful and competent, are never flashy, but the components of his songs mesh so well that the final product usually is highly successful.

Staines first picked up guitar at the age of 10 and taught himself to play it upside-down and backwards, Libba Cotten-style. He wrote his first song at 18 and, like many contemporary folk-style songwriters, he cites the folk performers of the 1960s—especially Ian Tyson and early Gordon Lightfoot—as the most significant influences on his music. Yet Staines's music is not imitative; if anything, it emulates traditional music while at the same time reflecting an aesthetic unmistakably his own.

Because he tries to write as many different kinds of songs as possible, his music encompasses a wide array of subjects: male-female relations, the seasons, travel, history, and legends. Although he hails from New England, a large body of his work concerns the American West—cowboys, rodeos, the Gold Rush, and so on.

He deliberately looks for simple and pretty melodies that will stick in people's minds; Staines the performer likes having audiences sing along on the choruses to his songs. And much of his writing is, as a result, geared toward the live audiences he plays to much of the year.

He has a warm, pleasing voice, but his most striking vocal talent is yodeling. He was, in fact, U.S. National Yodeling Champion in 1975, and he often writes songs that showcase that particular talent.

Clearly Staines is equally at home in front of an audience and in a recording studio; he is, likewise, comfortable with traditional material and other people's songs along with his own compositions. Yet his writing remains paramount in his career. "More than anything I'm a songwriter," he once said, noting that songwriting is the way he communicates best.

S·E·L·E·C·T·E·D R·E·C·O·R·D·I·N·G·S

The Whistle of the Jay
(FOLK-LEGACY FSI-70)
•
Rodeo Rose
(PHILO 1079)

The Whistle of the Jay may well be Staines's best album so far, with simple arrangements of some of his best songs. Several, like "Roseville Fair," "A Place in the Choir," and the exquisite "River" have been picked up by other musicians, but Staines's own versions remain the best. *Rodeo Rose* is far more produced, but tastefully so, and "Prairie Song" and "Lovers and Losers" are especially memorable. Both albums are ample proof that Staines deserves far more attention than he's received to date.

RESOURCES
WHERE TO BUY FOLK MUSIC RECORDS

Chances are, the people at your neighborhood record store will look at you blankly if you ask for nearly any of the records listed in this book. Happily, there are a few excellent mail-order sources for such records.

In the United States, the best place to start is:

Down Home Music
10341 San Pablo Avenue, El Cerrito, CA 94530.

Friendly, knowledgeable staff, fair prices, fast, personalized service and a huge stock, sometimes even including out-of-print and hard-to-get records, all combine to make Down Home Music the best source of folk music and related records in the U.S. (They also ship overseas.) Their retail store is worth checking out anytime you're in the San Francisco area. Write to them to begin receiving their newsletter.

Other sources you might want to try include:

Alcazar Records
P.O. Box 82, RD 2
Waterbury, VT 05676

Andy's Front Hall
RD 1, Box 93
Vorheesville, NY 12186

Elderly Instruments
541 East Grand River
P.O. Box 1795
East Lansing, MI 48823

Roundup Records
P.O. Box 147
East Cambridge, MA 02141

IN BRITAIN:

Dragon Records
5 Church Street,
Aylesbury,
Buckinghamshire

Dobell's Folk Record Shop
21 Tower Street
London, WC2H 9NS

Folk Shop
Cecil Sharp House
2 Regents Park Road
London, NW1 7AY

Projection Records
74 High Street
Old Town,
Leight-on-Sea, Essex

FOLK MUSIC PUBLICATIONS

U.S.:
Come for to Sing
917 W. Wolfram
Chicago, IL 60657

ENGLAND:
The Southern Rag
2 Eastdale, East St.
Farnham Surrey, GU9 7TB

Swing 51
41 Bushey Road
Sutton Surrey SM1 1QR

OTHER SOURCES

If you're after additional information, the Archive of Folk Culture at the Library of Congress in Washington, D.C., regularly publishes listings of record labels specializing in folk music, folk music periodicals, record distributors, folk clubs, and virtually anything else you can think of relating to North American folk music.

In England, the English Folk Dance and Song Society at Cecil Sharp House, 2 Regents Park Road, London, NW1 7AY, provides similar information.

INDEX